INSIDER
JESUS

THEOLOGICAL REFLECTIONS ON
NEW CHRISTIAN MOVEMENTS

William A. Dyrness

IVP Academic

An imprint of InterVarsity Press
Downers Grove, Illinois

InterVarsity Press
P.O. Box 1400, Downers Grove, IL 60515-1426
ivpress.com
email@ivpress.com

InterVarsity Press® is the book-publishing division of InterVarsity Christian Fellowship/USA®, a movement of students and faculty active on campus at hundreds of universities, colleges and schools of nursing in the United States of America, and a member movement of the International Fellowship of Evangelical Students. For information about local and regional activities, visit intervarsity.org.

Scripture quotations, unless otherwise noted, are from the New Revised Standard Version of the Bible, copyright 1989 by the Division of Christian Education of the National Council of the Churches of Christ in the USA. Used by permission. All rights reserved.

While any stories in this book are true, some names and identifying information may have been changed to protect the privacy of individuals.

Cover design: Cindy Kiple
Interior design: Daniel van Loon
Images: stone doorway: Sthaporn/iStockphoto
mosque entrance: robertharding/Fotolia.com
monastery doorway: f9photos/Fotolia.com

ISBN 978-0-8308-5155-3 (print)
ISBN 978-0-8308-7316-6 (digital)

Printed in the United States of America ∞

Library of Congress Cataloging-in-Publication Data
A catalog record for this book is available from the Library of Congress.

P 25 24 23 22 21 20 19 18 17 16 15 14 13 12 11 10 9 8 7 6 5 4 3 2 1

Y 37 36 35 34 33 32 31 30 29 28 27 26 25 24 23 22 21 20 19 18 17 16

"When we are confronted with the reality of religious pluralism, genuine struggles and dialogues are possible only if we take our own faith seriously and at the same time deeply respect the truth claims of other faiths. Professor Dyrness's creation of hermeneutical spaces makes such struggles and dialogues not only possible but, indeed, imperative. A must-read for anyone yearning to learn more about God's mission in the world today."

Sze-kar Wan, professor of New Testament, Perkins School of Theology, Southern Methodist University

"At last we have in this work an attempt by a Western theologian to understand and truly locate, within our contexts as non-Western Christian peoples, the ongoing work of the Spirit in so-called insider movements. The rise of insider movements is a challenge to recognize the fresh work of the Christ outside of the territorial and theological boundaries of 'Christendom.' In a way, we are seeing a reprise of the Jew-Gentile social crisis—those critical times when the gospel broke out of its Jewish wineskins and the early Greek converts had to grope about as to its life-changing meaning within their own worldview systems. It is providential that at this juncture of the history of the churches, we have fellow travelers like the author of this book to accompany us and shed some light along the way."

Melba Padilla Maggay, Institute for Studies in Asian Church and Culture

"This book is groundbreaking. Conversations have been taking place questioning the ongoing value of the contextualization movement. This is because among evangelicals contextualization has largely been a project conducted by outsiders assisting those who are insiders. This was an essential step in missions, yet the limitations of the movement are obvious. What is exciting is that in our postcolonial era new theological discourses and practices are emerging from within believing communities that seek to be faithful to Scripture and address more specifically and resonate more deeply with the worlds of these communities. Dyrness lucidly and sensitively introduces the reader to these developments and provides the reader with the theological and conceptual categories to understand and appreciate them."

Patrick Krayer, executive director, Interserve USA

"*Insider Jesus*, written by one of the foremost theologians of culture, makes a significant contribution to the growing body of works on global theology. It seeks to move beyond the current models of contextualization, which tend to privilege the outsider's (missionary) understanding of the gospel at the expense of the insider's. It advocates an 'intercultural theology' that involves older Christian traditions engaging in serious dialogue with the newer expressions of the Christian faith in indigenous movements. The result is not only mutual enrichment but perhaps a new kind of ecumenicity from which a genuinely evangelical-catholic faith would eventually emerge. Protestants and especially evangelicals need to read this book!"

Simon Chan, Trinity Theological College, Singapore

"In a day when many too quickly give a thumbs-up or thumbs-down response to new movements of followers of Jesus who try to retain much of their religious and cultural heritage of birth, this study offers a wealth of biblical, historical, and theological insight to help us all give a more informed and constructive response."

J. Dudley Woodberry, dean emeritus and senior professor of Islamic studies, School of Intercultural Studies, Fuller Theological Seminary

"As the growth in emergent insider movements continues unabated across the globe, missiologists have begun to grapple with the theological and missiological implications of these movements for global Christianity. What does it mean for subaltern communities to embrace Jesus and his gospel while remaining institutionally rooted within their own religious communities? Drawing on biblical, theological, and ethnographic resources, William A. Dyrness's *Insider Jesus* offers a comprehensive, critical, and constructive theological response to the challenges arising from the continuing growth of emergent insider movements across the globe. This response truly embraces the plurality of hybridized, boundary-crossing, and transreligious ways in which believers have chosen to follow Jesus while maintaining existing social ties, cultural identities, and religious belongings. As the culmination and crowning achievement of Dyrness's lifelong journey as a missioner and missiologist across Asia, Africa, and Latin America, this compelling and indispensable book is destined to be a seminal resource for missiologists and missioners that is biblically sound and theologically rigorous, yet clear and engaging for nonspecialist readers. I have no hesitation in recommending this as essential reading for scholars and students of Christian mission and global evangelism alike."

Jonathan Y. Tan, Archbishop Paul J. Hallinan Professor of Catholic Studies, Case Western Reserve University, Cleveland

CONTENTS

PREFACE

For some time now there has been a quiet revolution going on in Christian missions. In mainline and Roman Catholic missions one might point to the 1960s as the critical turning point; for evangelicals one might call attention to the Lausanne Conference or the Willowbank Consultation in the 1970s. At that point the changes were represented by terms like *inculturation* or, for evangelicals, *contextualization*. This called attention to the increasing—socioeconomic, cultural, even political—diversity of places where missionaries worked, and the necessity of adjusting their methods to this pluralism. But there were more surprises to come. Sometime around the turn of the century Western Christians awakened to the fact that, contrary to what they had assumed, Christianity was no longer simply a Western religion. Indeed, the Western part of it was a distinct (and often diminishing) minority; its "heartlands" were more likely to be Dalit communities in India or the favelas of Rio de Janeiro than the suburbs of midwestern America. And since September 11, 2001, a whole new dimension of this diversity has come dramatically to our attention: the newly awakened religious identities in which global Christianity now has to find its way.

This book makes no attempt to describe or analyze this revolution, but it does attend to one critical dimension of it, specifically the many insider and emergent movements that have appeared in the last generation. These call attention to a single inescapable aspect of the new situation: not only is there a wide diversity of people who name the name of Christ, but many of these have become agents of Christian mission in their own right. Though often invisible to Western Christians, and independent of external support, they have set off with Christ on a journey of discovery. Their witness and their vernacular theologies, much to the dismay of Western observers, necessarily reflect their various, and widely different, indigenous religious traditions and political situations. To further complicate matters, though these groups were earlier objects of Western missions, for various cultural, religious, or political reasons they now frequently resist the forms of Christianity they have inherited. They are emphatically postcolonial and post-Christendom—even if these may be foreign terms to them.

What are we to make of this new situation? The typical evangelical response to such changes is to hold consultations and develop grand strategies and complicated tactics to address the new situation. In other words, the response is consistently on the level of contextualization. I argue here that contextualization language—and the projects growing out of this—needs to be radically revised to properly engage the current proliferation of emergent and insider movements, and appropriately reflect on their significance.

In many ways I feel inadequate addressing such a complex and fraught subject. Though I am a former missionary with long experience teaching in Asia and Africa, and strong personal and professional association with Latin America, I have no direct experience with insider groups. But the happy experience of working alongside colleagues at Fuller Seminary, in the Philippines, in Kenya, and beyond has exposed me to some of the significant voices in this movement, and I have been drawn to the questions they have raised. As a theologian of culture, I have been struck by the importance of cultural diversity and the influence of this on religious developments today. It seems these two interrelated realities—growing cultural pluralism and newly aroused religious identities—call not simply for new missionary programs but, in the first instance, for deep theological reflection, something the discussion of this book seeks to promote. The question I want to ask is, what might God be doing and intending in this new global religious world? Only after considering this question should we ask how we might respond to this in modest and appropriate ways.

This book would never have been begun apart from close colleagues, students (and former students), and friends who together are observing and assessing this new situation of mission and have stimulated my thinking. At Fuller I am extremely grateful for the support of John Jay Travis, Dan Shaw, Dudley Woodberry, Martin Acad, Robert Johnston, Veli-Matti Karkkainen,

Amos Yong, Joel Green, Cory Willson, and Oscar Garcia-Johnson. Jay, who is himself one of the important early observers of these movements, was especially kind to share with me a prepublication version of the massive *Understanding Insider Movements*, which has collected many of the critical articles and chapters addressing insider movements.[1] Darren Duerksen, professor at Fresno Pacific University, has taught me much about emergent movements. His published dissertation has been a crucial source.[2] Darren, John Goldingay, Roger Hedlund, and Robert Hubbard made helpful comments on the manuscript. Colleagues in the Philippines, at Asian Theological Seminary and the Institute for Studies in Asian Church and Culture—especially Dr. Melba Maggay, Professor Lorenzo Bautista, Dr. Adonis Gorospe, and Dr. Timoteo Gener, joined earlier by Kang-San Tan—were conversation partners when the idea of this book was birthed in September 2014 in Manila. Also helpful in thinking through issues in Asia, along with Kang-San Tan, have been Jonathan Tan and Father Joseph Cheah. In Nairobi, at the Africa International University, Dean James Nkansah-Obrempong and PhD students Jacob Kimathi Samuel and Josephine Munyao have been indispensible friends and theological sources. Editors Dan Reid and David Congdon have been an encouragement throughout. David was especially helpful, along with an anonymous reviewer, in prodding me to clarify my argument. The book is sent forth with the prayer that it will stimulate not only thought but also concerted prayer and support for the new things God is doing around the world.

---

[1]Cf. Harley Talman and John Jay Travis, eds., *Understanding Insider Movements: Disciples of Jesus Within Diverse Religious Communities* (Pasadena, CA: William Carey Library, 2015).
[2]See Darren Todd Duerksen, *Ecclesial Identities in a Multi-Faith Context: Jesus Truth-Gatherings (Yeshu Satsangs) Among Hindus and Sikhs in Northwest India* (Eugene, OR: Pickwick, 2015).

CHAPTER ONE

INTRODUCTION
The Rise of Contextualization

Christ plays in ten thousand places,
Lovely in limbs, and lovely in eyes not his
To the Father through the features of men's faces.

GERARD MANLEY HOPKINS

Hardly anything has proven more contentious in recent years than the proliferation of new forms of church and mission within non-Christian religions and religious cultures, and even within Christianity itself—so-called emergent or insider ecclesial forms. They are often maligned by prominent figures both in Christianity and in these other religions. Seen from another angle, hardly anything is more interesting and promising than to imagine that God might be doing a new thing in these contexts. Specifically I have in mind movements among people in Islam who call themselves Muslim believers in *Isa al Masih* ("Jesus" in Arabic); these have appeared in Bangladesh and many places in Southeast Asia. There are also Hindu and Sikh followers of Jesus called *Yeshu Satsangs* (Jesus Gatherings), small groups in North India who seek to stay in their Sikh or Hindu communities. Movements of this kind have been called insider movements, which are defined by Scott Moreau as "movements to obedient faith in Christ that remain integrated with or *inside* their natural community."[1]

---

[1]A. Scott Moreau, *Contextualization in World Missions: Mapping and Assessing Evangelical Models* (Grand Rapids: Kregel, 2012), 161, emphasis original.

Meanwhile, many Christians in non-Christian settings are exploring ways to encourage faith practices that are more sensitive to longstanding cultural practices that have traditionally divided families and communities. Here one might note Christian groups in Japan seeking new ways to think about ancestor veneration or Christians in Buddhist countries who are paying visits to the temples with their families. Responsible consideration of these many efforts is complicated by the fact that many—indeed most—of these groups must remain hidden from the (religious and political) authorities, so reliable information is difficult or impossible to attain. Still they call out for attention.

This book is not meant to be primarily a description or evaluation of these movements—though a later chapter will include several substantial case studies; rather, it seeks to provide a theological perspective for thinking about them. Better, since no single theological framework can claim to make sense of such diverse movements, it will attempt to begin a theological conversation about these developments that attends to Scripture and is sensitive to the place of these movements in the long history of the Christian church.

It is not hard to see why so-called insider movements are threatening to many Christians. They relate centrally to the person and work of Christ, and they raise questions about the nature of the community that he intended to gather in his name. Indeed, in the end they touch on the nature of the salvation that God promised to the Jewish people in the First Testament and that the apostles claim was revealed in Jesus, whom they called the Christ. Though these are, in the end, critical issues, it strikes me that dealing directly with them is the wrong way to go about addressing, especially, the controversial aspects of these movements. For what underlies these concerns are conflicting cultural codes and multiple conceptions of religion, and it is here I think that the conversation should begin. Even here, I will argue, theological issues are at stake that I want to track down and highlight.

Let me provide explanation for this approach by way of a personal introduction. Though I have taught and worked for many years in Asia (in the Philippines) and later in Africa and have family and professional connections in Latin America, I am an evangelical from the American Midwest who has studied theology in Europe and in America. In other words, my perspective has been formed inevitably by the cultural conditions and the theological conversations prevailing in Europe and America. Since I am not a party to any of the cultural settings of the insider movements I will describe, it would be inappropriate of me to seek to make theological judgments of them. But having reflected for many years on the settings in which theology is done, I want to consider these new movements to see what we might learn from them. To do this, I will suggest ways that multiple contexts and religious diversity provide hermeneutical spaces where new understandings of the gospel can emerge.

Another way of approaching this is to point out that from the beginning of the Christian movement there has been a wide variety of settings in which different versions of Christianity have emerged. Antioch provided a different sensitivity from Alexandria; later, Roman and Germanic voices were added. In the course of time, diverging sensitivities in the Eastern and Western churches proved so difficult that they had to go their separate ways, and later the Western church itself was divided—culturally as well as theologically—by the Reformation. These different settings did not always pick up the same themes from Scripture, and, though the divisions were frequently painful, Christianity is richer for this diversity. Meanwhile, since the time of the sixteenth-century Reformation, cultural and religious pluralism has become even more prominent and more inescapable. Many scholars have pointed out that the variety of situations that Christianity inhabits today in many ways recalls the early period of Christianity and calls for similar sensitivity. As David Smith argues, from the beginning of the Christian church, cross-cultural (and, we might add, interreligious) encounters have facilitated the learning experience of the church.[2]

In the past, Christianity's adaptation to diverse settings has been characterized as contextualization. However, I would argue that a new appreciation and appropriation of difference suggests that the language of contextualization needs fresh examination. Thinking of missions in terms of how the gospel is contextualized represents a revolution in the understanding of mission, and this has been an indispensible step in encouraging thoughtful adaptation of the gospel to new settings. But I will argue that it does not always help us think about the new situation of interreligious encounter, in general, and of insider and other emergent Christian movements, in particular. Contextualization

---

[2]David Smith, *Mission After Christendom* (London: Darton, Longman & Todd, 2003), 53. And see Philip Jenkins, *The Next Christendom: The Coming of Global Christianity*, 3rd ed. (New York: Oxford University Press, 2011).

language, after all, has been developed and primarily directed at missionaries and evangelists who seek to communicate the gospel; now a variety of new actors have arisen that find this language inadequate. Traditional understandings of contextualization as a movement of Christianity into new settings have proven unhelpful for two reasons. First, these new efforts do not represent an intervention from without but give evidence of an indigenous impulse—that is, new forms are not suggested by outsiders; they are emerging from within. And, second, contextualization does not adequately capture the hermeneutical and dialogical character of mission whereby various accounts of God's presence (or that of the gods or spirits) are exchanged and evaluated.

The remaining part of this chapter will seek to elaborate these points. First, I will provide a brief sketch of the development of contextualization, especially since the 1960s. Second, I will note the problems that our current global situation has posed for the program of contextualization and what kind of conversation might be (and has been) proposed to replace it. The chapters that follow will seek to develop this suggestion. The second chapter will offer a brief theological perspective on culture growing out of God's purposes for creation and the re-creative work of Christ. Describing the human wisdom that culture represents, both in Scripture and in subsequent human history, I will argue, prepares us to think about religion and emerging forms of Christian mission in new ways. In the third chapter I turn our attention directly to religion, and specifically to the depiction of religion in the biblical narrative. I will seek to discover what God's purposes might be for religion. With a special focus on Paul's discourse on Mars Hill in Acts 17, I will recall how early Christians came to terms with the multireligious world they inherited and how they saw the Spirit of God working in surprising ways. The fourth chapter will provide some case studies that will allow us to explore ways that current movements either confirm or challenge the theological framework I have developed. The purpose of these studies is to see possible ways that God may be working both within Christianity today and in other religious settings. In chapter five, on the basis of these case studies, I will seek to develop a more nuanced view of religions as hermeneutical spaces that reflect unique cultural and geographic settings, and I will consider the implications of this for mission. A consideration of the variety of religious practices, and taking some time to look at Islam in particular, I will argue, provides resources for discerning the working of the Spirit in insider movements. My conclusion will suggest ways that this conversation might be pursued further and address what these reflections might entail for theological reflections on the church—what in theology is called ecclesiology.

REFORMATION, ENLIGHTENMENT, AND RELIGION: THE HISTORICAL CONTEXT

Since it is important to my argument that the inherited discourse of contextualization, especially as this is proposed in evangelical circles, needs to be revised to meet the challenges associated with insider and emerging ecclesial communities, it is appropriate to begin with a very brief review. In many ways, Christians have been thinking about these concerns since the beginning of the church. Indeed, much of the interaction in the book of Acts, both among the apostles and between them and nonbelievers, can be read as a kind of contextualization *avant la lettre*. The difficulty of seeking to make the gospel understood in the variety of settings around the world and throughout Christian history has been a constant concern for evangelists and missionaries. But discussions of contextualizing the gospel in the many cultures of the world, at least in North America, really only began in the last hundred years with the rise and influence of the social sciences. The conversation with which we are concerned began formally in the 1960s with the emphasis on inculturation growing out of the Second Vatican Council (1961–1965) in the Catholic Church.[3] But before I describe this development I want to return to an earlier period of Christian history.

For my purposes the critical point in the discussion lies neither in the twentieth century nor in the first but in the sixteenth. For it was in the sixteenth century that critical shifts in the understanding of religion took place that predetermined how the conversation about contextualization would eventually unfold more recently. Let me try to summarize what these changes were and why they were significant. Since issues of culture are central to my argument, it is important to remember that the changes instituted by the magisterial reformers were not *primarily* changes in beliefs but changes in practices

---

[3]We must be careful, however, of assuming that we have nothing to learn from the many previous attempts to explain and interpret the gospel. For example, Frank Laubach was known to encourage Muslim believers in Christ, initially at least, to remain in the mosque. See Frank C. Laubach, *The People of the Philippines: Their Religious Progress and Preparation for Spiritual Leadership in the Far East* (New York: George Doran, 1925).

that reflected both their rereading of Scripture and, also and more substantially, their changing cultural and historical situation.[4] Another way of putting this is to suggest that rather than changing belief, the Reformation changed the role and significance of belief, resulting in new ways of practicing religion.

How is this so? Between medieval Christianity and the Reformation, the average person would have noticed primarily a change from a familiar and longstanding set of practices—praying with images of the saints or rosaries, processions and pilgrimages, novenas, and so forth—to an emphasis on specific beliefs embodied in a new set of practices—preaching, learning catechisms, and reading Scripture and prayer books. The focus of worship was no longer the dramatic celebration of the Mass but the clear preaching of the Word of God. For ordinary believers this was facilitated not only by hearing sermons but also by learning the catechism and, eventually, reading Scripture for themselves. The resulting focus of religious devotion was thus transferred from external objects and practices to internal reflection and faith. Whereas in the medieval period the whole person, and all the senses, was involved in the performance of devotion, after the Reformation the head and heart became the primary focus.[5]

While Protestants, looking back, tend to assume that these changes were necessary, indeed in some ways were inevitable, this is not so. As many now recognize, despite the polemics of the Reformers, there was nothing intrinsically superstitious or idolatrous about many of the medieval practices. Indeed, for many Protestants monastic practices and medieval forms of prayer and Scripture reading (e.g., lectio divina) have experienced something of a revival. Nevertheless, it is important to understand the significance of the change of focus not only for understandings of God and salvation but also for conceptions of religion itself. Since the emphasis was placed almost

---

[4]It is the major flaw of Brad Gregory's otherwise important book that he does not recognize the role that these changing cultural circumstances played in the Reformation, seeing, as he does, the breakup of the medieval moral community as an unrelieved disaster. See Brad S. Gregory, *The Unintended Reformation: How a Religious Revolution Secularized Society* (Cambridge, MA: Harvard University Press, 2012).

[5]The contrasting characterization of these periods is that of Edward Muir, who provides a helpful summary of this development in *Ritual in Early Modern Europe* (Cambridge: Cambridge University Press, 1997). I have explored this transformation for Reformed Protestants in particular in William A. Dyrness, *Reformed Theology and Visual Culture: The Protestant Imagination from Calvin to Edwards* (Cambridge: Cambridge University Press, 2004).

entirely on the *break* with older practices, in the polemic environment of the century the way was open to contrast medieval superstition with the "true religion" of the Reformation.

For Protestants of course, and for this author in particular, the changes are perceived as mostly positive and have resulted in much that is good. But, for purposes of this discussion, it is also important to recognize what was lost. Much of the religious culture of medieval practice, and of monastic spirituality in particular, was swept away. The resources of the mystical tradition were disparaged, and rich traditions of material culture—of architecture, painting, and drama, to name only the most prominent—were mostly set aside. But more important for the argument of this book, a dramatic change occurred in the way "religion" was construed. Instead of providing a holistic frame that determined an entire way of life, including the political and social structure, religion was on the way to becoming an inward and personal (and often an individual) affair. This did not happen all at once, but over time this inward and personal faith was to become the default view of religion in the modern period, at least in the West. Again, this view of religion seems natural to us. But for many people outside the West, this understanding of religion appears strange, even incomprehensible. As a result, though this is seldom acknowledged, Western Christians find it difficult to have meaningful religious conversations across religious boundaries. Talal Asad, for example, has called attention to the deep affinity between medieval forms of Christianity and contemporary Islam, and to the vast differences of both in contrast to modern Western assumptions. Consider one prominent example that Asad develops. Modern views of freedom, which we take for granted, in which individuals freely choose their own religious pathways, contrast sharply with both medieval Christianity and Islam. These two traditions were agreed that virtue is formed in the context of moral communities *before* proper choices can be made.[6] Modern understandings of religion in the West work from very different assumptions.

---

[6]See Talal Asad, *Genealogies of Religion: Discipline and Reasons of Power in Christianity and Islam* (Baltimore: Johns Hopkins University Press, 1994). See chap. 4, "On Discipline and Humility in Medieval Christian Monasticism." On this point Brad Gregory's argument has merit: what was lost at the Reformation, he claims, at least in its more popular forms, was the understanding of a moral teleology that is formed within a larger moral community. See Gregory, *Unintended Reformation*, chap. 4.

While in fact much of the communal sense of morality, and certain patterns of worship, survived in the Reformation, in the dangerous and polemic environment of the time this continuity was mostly not recognized, and the entire medieval period was seen as a period of superstition and idolatry. It is not hard to see that some of these attitudes have survived into the modern period and color our attitudes toward other religions. Modern Protestants, especially evangelicals, are still likely to argue that their faith represents the truth about things and are therefore opposed to formalized religion in all its many forms (something we explore further in chapter three below).

But notice what happened when this Protestant form of the faith was taken to the nations of the world in the missionary movement. The focus on reading, interpreting, and preaching Scripture led to many positive elements in the missionary movement. Missionaries valued language and frequently pioneered translation of Scripture (and often important indigenous literature) into the language of the people. Indeed, Lamin Sanneh has argued that translation is a key category that helps us understand how the gospel came to take root in various (non-Western) cultures.[7] The positive impact of this on educational and medical developments where missionaries served is well documented.[8]

But there were other less positive outcomes from this emphasis on teaching and learning that Willie Jennings and others have recently highlighted. Since the understanding of the gospel was tied to a particular set of beliefs that resulted from Reformation Christianity, missionaries were insistent on making these beliefs clear—contextualizing them—in the places (and languages) where they worked. Jennings argues that this resulted in an "inverted hospitality," by which missionaries, rather than accepting the hospitality of host people and learning from their ways, were mostly intent on teaching—more anxious to impart the truth as they saw it than willing to learn from indigenous wisdom. There were many exceptions of course, and there is much to commend in their teaching practices, but there was a consonant danger in what Jennings calls the "pedagogical imagination" that still infects conversations about

---

[7]See Lamin Sanneh, *Translating the Message: The Missionary Impact on Culture* (Maryknoll, NY: Orbis Books, 1989).

[8]And has received renewed attention in Robert D. Woodberry, "The Missionary Roots of Liberal Democracy," *American Political Science Review* 106 (May 2012): 244-74.

insider movements.[9] And it also reflects widely different assumptions about the nature of religion.

There were other factors at work as well. The Reformers also inherited assumptions about the superiority of Christian culture, even if they differed on the form that culture should take. And they bequeathed these assumptions in the form of insensitivity to indigenous traditions. As Jehu Hanciles argues, the Protestant mission, when it finally got off the ground two hundred years after the Reformation, left intact the underlying construct of Christendom. "The Western missionary enterprise was marked by the dye of Christendom in its fundamental assumptions, operational strategy and long-term objectives."[10] By this he means that the missionary program was often allied with territorial expansion, pursued with the collaboration of political authorities, and framed in terms of spreading Christian civilization around the world.[11]

But even here, I would argue, the Reformation focus on language and belief played a decisive role. The developing focus on a particular belief structure, especially as this was elaborated by Protestant scholasticism, surely encouraged a particular intellectual imperialism that was inclined to pay little attention to indigenous wisdom. The emotional center of non-Western people is often expressed in stories, myths, and legends; it is articulated in dances, cult objects, and music that embody what the people love. These elements were often suppressed on the grounds that they expressed idolatrous beliefs but also because such cultural forms were felt to be inferior to more cognitive forms of meaning making. This external dimension of culture—its rituals and images—had been devalued and mostly discarded when the sixteenth-century Reformers sought to purify the church.

In the Enlightenment that swept through Europe (and later America) in the eighteenth and nineteenth centuries, these changes were both canonized and secularized. When René Descartes sat alone in his darkened room and

---

[9]Willie James Jennings, *The Christian Imagination: Theology and the Origins of Race* (New Haven, CT: Yale University Press, 2010), 109-12.

[10]Jehu Hanciles, *Beyond Christendom: Globalization, African Migration and the Transformation of the West* (Maryknoll, NY: Orbis Books, 2008), 96. Hanciles here is borrowing the well-known argument of Kenneth Latourette that the Reformation may actually have encouraged convictions about Christendom. But one could challenge this by noting that, while this initially may have been true, the processes that I am tracing would eventually challenge this structure.

[11]There were important critiques of this colonialism: one thinks of William Carey in India and Bartolomé de las Casas in Latin America.

concluded that only his own thinking was indubitable—*cogito, ergo sum* (I think, therefore I am)—he could not have imagined what a gulf he was creating between Western and non-Western ways of thinking. If thinking is the primary locus of truth, all other embodied cultural forms must surely be inferior. Many students I have taught in Africa and Asia have found this reversal of things difficult to understand.

The scholar who first described these momentous changes with respect to religion was Wilfred Cantwell Smith in his classic 1962 book on *The Meaning and End of Religion*. The modern notion of religion, he argued, is based on the intellectualist and impersonal schematization of things that resulted from the Enlightenment. He wrote:

> In pamphlet after pamphlet, treatise after treatise, decade after decade the notion was driven home that a religion is something one believes or does not believe, something whose propositions are true or are not true, something whose *locus* is in the realm of the intelligible, is up for speculation before the speculative mind.[12]

Smith saw this as a result of Reformation ideas as these were developed by the scholasticism of the succeeding centuries. This means, he noted, that religion had become not something that is to be done but something that is believed. The way was open to understand belief in purely rational and often abstract terms. This construal of religion, he argued, when compared with widely different views elsewhere, makes the use of *religion* as a noun problematic; he proposed *faith* and *cumulative tradition*, respectively, for the subjective and objective aspects of religion. Though written more than half a century ago, Smith's formulation has sparked new attention in the current conversation.

Recently, in reflecting on his book after forty years, Smith noted that though he had grasped the role of the Enlightenment in defining religion, he had not seen that religion itself was an essentially secular notion. As he came to see it, secularism is an ideology, and

> religion is one of its basic categories. . . . It sees the universe and human nature, as essentially secular, and sees "the religions" as addenda that human beings have tacked on here and there in various shapes and for various . . . reasons. It

---

[12]Wilfred Cantwell Smith, *The Meaning and End of Religion: A New Approach to the Religious Traditions of Mankind* (New York: Macmillan, 1962), 40. The result is the tendency to ask people, what do you believe?—as though this were *the* basic question.

sees law, economics, philosophy (things we got from Greece and Rome) as distinct from religion.[13]

While this isolation of religion from other areas of life is assumed in the West, it makes little sense in many other places.

In chapter five I will draw out the implications of these changes for understanding religion, but here I highlight their significance for the discussion of contextualization. On the one hand, it is important to remember that many parts of Africa and Asia have no cultural experience or memory of the events associated with the Enlightenment (or for that matter the Reformation). They work out of a different cultural memory, with wholly different assumptions. We Western Christians, on the other hand, cannot escape this history; it is part of the intellectual air we breathe. Moreover, we often unconsciously apply its lessons in normative ways, and one of those ways is our insistence on the need to formulate the gospel in very specific terms, as this has been distilled from our reading of Scripture and shaped by our particular theological tradition. This picture of our Christian faith necessarily colors our understanding of Christian mission and the need to contextualize, into various cultural situations, a particular set of beliefs about what God has done in Christ.

TWENTIETH CENTURY: FROM CONTEXTUALIZATION TO LOCAL THEOLOGY

Major changes that took place during the last century reflected a growing social-scientific awareness and an increased pluralism associated with late modern globalization. The former may be represented by the work of Franz Boas (1858–1942), who introduced the notion of ethnography.[14] Resisting the reigning paradigm that all cultures progress along a single evolutionary path, Boas proposed empirical and inductive methods that sought to let the

---

[13]Wilfred Cantwell Smith, "Retrospective Thoughts on *The Meaning and End of Religion*," in *Religion in History: The Word, the Idea, the Reality*, ed. Michel Despland and Gérard Vallée (Waterloo, Ont.: Wilfred Laurier University Press, 1992), 16. Quoted and discussed in H. L. Richard, "Religious Syncretism as a Syncretistic Concept: The Inadequacy of the 'World Religions' Paradigm in Cross-Cultural Encounter," in *Understanding Insider Movements: Disciples of Jesus Within Diverse Religious Communities*, ed. Harley Talman and John Jay Travis (Pasadena, CA: William Carey Library, 2015), 367. As Richard notes, this is not to say there were no positive results from the Enlightenment, particularly in the area of religious tolerance.

[14]Franz Boas, *The Ethnography of Franz Boas*, comp. and ed. Ronald P. Rohner (Chicago: University of Chicago Press, 1969), xvi, xxiii. Rohner points out that Boas did more to develop and refine the notion of American ethnography than to introduce new ideas (p. xxx).

people speak for themselves. Especially interesting was his focus not on what people do but on what they say they do or feel they should do, which helped researchers see the world from the indigenous point of view. Boas's accounts are full of rich descriptions of the carvings and paintings of the people and the songs and dances that accompanied their festive meals. Among the many virtues associated with his understanding of ethnography is the attention that was paid not only to what came to be called *worldviews* (which maintained the focus we are underlining on cognitive analysis) but even more to the careful description of social patterns and to practices of art and religion (which are often deeply interrelated). It was in this broader world of practices, Boas and others discovered, that people forged their identities.

Happily, many missionaries trained since the 1970s have had the benefit of understanding the richness of cultural practices and the ways in which these often have religious roots and meaning. As noted earlier, the modern conversation of contextualization began in the 1960s with what was called in Catholic circles *inculturation*. From the beginning of its impetus in the Second Vatican Council, the emphasis has been on understanding, not how the gospel can be "understood" in the various settings where it is preached (the Protestant focus) but on how the church and its sacramental practices might find a home—how these might be inculturated—in those places. Putting things this way helps us see that for Catholics the cultural practices were immediately seen as possible allies in the attempt to evangelize a people—something that has often sparked suspicion on the part of their Protestant colleagues.

Around this time conversations about the indigenization of Christianity became popular, and in 1972 Shoki Coe coined the term *contextualization*.[15] Evangelical interest in contextualization was triggered by these discussions, but it did not find traction until the Lausanne Congress on Evangelism in 1974. There for the first time voices from what was then called the "Third World" were raised in support of alternative expressions of the gospel within an overall kingdom framework. These initiatives were further developed in the famous Willowbank Conference, which produced a widely influential collection of essays edited by John R. W. Stott and Robert Coote.[16]

---

[15]See Shoki Coe, *Recollections and Reflections* (New York: Formosan Christians for Self-Determination, 1993).

[16]John R. W. Stott and Robert T. Coote, *Down to Earth: Essays in Gospel and Culture* (Grand Rapids: Eerdmans, 1980). Though influential, this volume did not solve a simmering debate about the

During the 1980s and 1990s a gradual shift was taking place in Christian reflection on culture. Again, developments in social science proved to be influential. Already in the 1970s Clifford Geertz published his highly influential *The Interpretation of Cultures*.[17] This was a helpful way to see religion as including practices and symbolic objects as well as beliefs. But, as Talal Asad has pointed out, Geertz's was more a "Protestant" reading of culture than a religiously neutral one.[18] What mattered were the ideas embodied in the symbols rather than the symbols and practices themselves. Geertz's influence soon became apparent when missiologists began to make use of his emphasis on religion as a symbolic system of practices and beliefs, allowing them to interpret contextualization in more nuanced ways. In 1979 Bruce Nicholls argued that contextualization was an advance over older ideas of indigenization because it was able to take account of more complex social processes.[19] And that same year Charles Kraft published his influential *Christianity in Culture*. Making use of Geertz's understanding of religion within a communication model, Kraft described theologizing as a dynamic discovery process.[20]

In the 1980s a new wave of anthropological reflection dramatically changed the focus of the conversation. In an important 1984 article, Sherry B. Ortner argued that individuals are not passively determined by cultural influences: they are agents; they have the ability to make something of their situation.[21] Ortner argued that culture embodies "serious games" in which persons and groups can resist and even transform cultural norms. This had enormous significance for thinking about missionary strategy because it suggested that readers of newly translated Scriptures were capable of interpreting them on their own terms, and that such readings could become culturally

---

varying importance of evangelism and social concern that has often preoccupied evangelical missiologists and colored discussions of contextualization.

[17] Clifford Geertz, *The Interpretation of Cultures: Selected Essays* (New York: Basic Books, 1973).

[18] See Asad, *Genealogies of Religion*, chapter one. Asad's point is that the symbols are simply objects that embody and point to what the person considers reality. That is, what counts are the ideas behind the symbols. But, Asad notes, for Islam (and for medieval monastic spirituality) the practices themselves carry the analytic weight.

[19] Bruce J. Nicholls, *Contextualization: A Theology of Gospel and Culture* (Downers Grove, IL: InterVarsity Press, 1979). I am grateful to David Congdon for reminding me of the Nicholls book.

[20] Charles H. Kraft, *Christianity in Culture: A Study of Dynamic Biblical Theologizing in Cross-Cultural Perspective* (Maryknoll, NY: Orbis Books, 1979), 56, 294. Interestingly, though Kraft describes the process, he does not use the term *contextualization*.

[21] Sherry B. Ortner, "Theory in Anthropology Since the Sixties," *Comparative Studies in Society and History* 26 (January 1984): 126-66.

transformative.[22] At about the same time, many were reading and learning from Hans-Georg Gadamer, who argued that cultural inheritances were not a handicap in understanding texts but actually provided lenses that enabled people to make sense of their world. With respect to the mission of the church, then, a people's effective history—including myths and stories—can become hermeneutical resources rather than barriers to the understanding of faith and the reading of Scripture.[23]

So the emphasis of the 1980s and 1990s shifted the focus from the messenger (and the message) to the hearers and their world—that is, the actual space they inhabit. The one who interpreted this sea change for missiology was David Bosch in his monumental *Transforming Mission* in 1991.[24] He argued that Jesus did not come to start a new religion or to assure the survival of an existing one but to call out a vanguard of a new people distinguished by calling and responsibility. In the course of time, however, "the Jesus community simply became a new religion, Christianity, a new principle of division among humankind. And so it has remained to this day."[25] Later in the book he draws out the implications for missiology while noting that, in contrast to the enfleshment of Buddhism, whose history displays a remarkable flexibility, Christian mission has often been one of disembodiment, thus undermining the essentially dialogical nature of the Christian mission.[26]

Robert Schreiter was a leading theorist in the changes this implied. Early on, like Bosch, he recognized the significance of Ortner's "turn to the subject," publishing an important book entitled *Constructing Local Theologies* in 1985.[27] And later he would argue that the increasingly globalized and interconnected world required that understanding both Christian truth and scriptural texts must now be an intercultural process.

Evangelicals during this period also began to recognize the importance of "reception" in the missionary program. In 1987 Paul Hiebert published an important article on "Critical Contextualization."[28] He acknowledged that

---

[22]This was of course the point that Lamin Sanneh was to make in his 1989 book, *Translating the Message*.

[23]See Hans-Georg Gadamer, *Truth and Method* (German ed., 1965; New York: Seabury, 1975).

[24]David J. Bosch, *Transforming Mission: Paradigm Shifts in Mission Theology* (Maryknoll, NY: Orbis Books, 1991), 50.

[25]Ibid., 477-78.

[26]Ibid., 483-84.

[27]Robert J. Schreiter, *Constructing Local Theologies* (Maryknoll, NY: Orbis Books, 1985).

[28]Paul G. Hiebert, "Critical Contextualization," *International Bulletin of Missionary Research* 11,

exegesis of culture must interact with our exegesis of Scripture—which he called the hermeneutical bridge. And he appropriately recognized the need for the people themselves to corporately evaluate their past, critically, in the light of their new biblical understanding. Though he acknowledged the need for new contextualized practices, emphasis still came to rest on the intellectual sorting of alternative frameworks.

A similar view was evident in the major work of David Hesselgrave and Edward Rommen published in 1989.[29] They argued that contextualization is necessary because the supercultural gospel must be dislodged from our own (i.e., the missionaries') culture while not allowing it to be syncretistically connected to aspects of other cultures that would compromise the message. As a result, they proposed an "orthodox didactic" model of contextualization that teaches truth—so that revelation will be understood as applied to the new situation—in the peoples' own language and ways of acting. While helpfully acknowledging the role of anthropological and hermeneutical models, Hesselgrave and Rommen held out for the need to balance faithfulness and meaningfulness. Though more weight was given to reception and to understanding the message, the emphasis was still on the appropriate communication of gospel truth.

Robert Schreiter pointed out the limitation of such an approach in his later book, *The New Catholicity*. He wrote:

> The speaker is concerned with getting a message across the cultural boundaries with integrity and lodging it in the world of the hearer in such a way that it will be understood. The hearer, on the other hand, is concerned with finding a place for that message within his or her own world in such a way as to enhance the hearer's identity.[30]

In other words, it is the messenger that is mostly concerned with the integrity of the message, rooted as this is in "true knowledge of God"; he or she is the one concerned with contextualization. Meanwhile, the hearer is concerned with more immediate issues connected to his or her very identity. And these

no. 3 (1987): 104-12. Reprinted in Hiebert, *Anthropological Reflections on Missiological Issues* (Grand Rapids: Baker Books, 1994), 75-92.

[29]David J. Hesselgrave and Edward Rommen, *Contextualization: Meanings, Methods and Models* (Grand Rapids: Baker Books, 1989). The reference to a supercultural gospel is from p. 1; see pp. 155, 199, and 206-7 for what follows.

[30]Robert J. Schreiter, *The New Catholicity: Theology Between the Global and the Local* (Maryknoll, NY: Orbis Books, 1997), 35.

identities are often rooted in deep-seated cultural and religious values and impulses. In other words, this process is from the very beginning a two-way exchange in which, I will argue, God is already an active participant.

FROM CONTEXTUALIZATION TO INTERCULTURAL THEOLOGY

This last comment brings us into the decades beginning in 2000, or more properly beginning with September 11, 2001, when we were painfully confronted with new forms of pluralism.[31] For it was then we realized that the future of the world was not only intercultural and global but also emphatically interreligious. By this time, voices had already called for rethinking contextualization,[32] and during this period the conversation was broadened in important ways. Two important books published in 2005 illustrate evangelical responses to some of these changes. Dean Flemming argues that the New Testament itself provides important guidance for thinking about Christian mission. Moving beyond communication models of contextualization, he contends that the New Testament unveils a "dynamic and comprehensive process by which the gospel is incarnated within a concrete historical or cultural situation."[33] Understood in this way, the New Testament provides a chorus of Spirit-inspired *contextualizations* (Flemming's term) of Christ's work, involving engagement that is both constructive and corrective, and that produces a welcome diversity of insights into the gospel.

A more substantial volume that appeared the same year, edited by Charles Kraft, pushes the discourse of contextualization in new directions. Kraft proposes that the goal of indigeneity is "doing whatever is necessary to make sure Christianity is expressed in ways that are appropriate to the context of the receiving group," and he goes on to describe the history of contextualization among evangelicals where "implementation has lapsed far behind the

---

[31]For the introduction of the term *intercultural theology*, see "Mission Studies as Intercultural Theology and Its Relation to Religious Studies," *Mission Studies* 25, no. 1 (2008). This statement by the Academic Association for Theology (WGTh) in Germany proposes intercultural theology as the primary discipline for the encounter between Christianity and non-Christian religions, replacing mission studies.

[32]For example, as early as 1994 Paul Hiebert had called for metatheology as a step beyond contextualization. See Paul G. Hiebert, "Metatheology: The Step Beyond Contextualization," in *Anthropological Reflections on Missiological Issues* (Grand Rapids: Baker Books, 1994), 93-103, in which Hiebert anticipates developments that were to come.

[33]Dean Flemming, *Contextualization in the New Testament: Patterns for Theology and Mission* (Downers Grove, IL: InterVarsity Press, 2005), 19.

conceptualization."[34] This collection is sensitive to the new pluralistic situation, in which, Paul E. Pierson asserts, God is "constantly taking the Gospel to groups and places often considered beyond the possibility of salvation" and where, Charles E. Van Engen observes, "Christian knowledge about God is seen as cumulative, enhanced, deepened, broadened and expanded as the Gospel takes shape in each new culture."[35] This means that future encounters, Van Engen argues, will be opportunities for Western and non-Western groups to learn from each other, in what he calls a "praxeological hermeneutical spiral."

During this period, there were also important movements in Western theology more generally that provide resources for our thinking about the movement of the gospel today. One such development, called "comparative theology," while primarily an academic conversation, has proposed ways of exploring other faith traditions while holding to one's own faith, in a way that facilitates mutual learning and correction. Francis X. Clooney, a leading voice in this movement, describes the discipline of comparative theology as "the practice of rethinking aspects of one's own faith tradition through the study of aspects of another faith tradition."[36] Beginning with (Western and non-Western) theological traditions, and largely motivated by more academic concerns, this movement has proposed a theological encounter that seeks to understand each other "thickly," in ways that appropriate the long histories of accumulated beliefs, practices, and moral sensitivities. This approach assumes that such encounters become spaces where fresh insights are possible, indebted both to the newly encountered faith and to the home tradition.[37]

---

[34]Charles H. Kraft, ed., *Appropriate Christianity* (Pasadena, CA: William Carey Library, 2005), 4, 31. Dedicated to missiologist Dean Gilliland, this volume includes papers from faculty and students of Fuller's School of Intercultural Studies; eleven of the twenty-eight chapters were contributed by Kraft.

[35]Paul E. Pierson, "Renewal, Revival and Contextualization," 441; Charles E. Van Engen, "Five Perspectives of Missional Theology," 197, 214; both in Kraft, *Appropriate Christianity*. Van Engen's chapter in *Appropriate Christianity* offers important clues about the reciprocal nature of mission theology and the role of practices that I will explore in what follows.

[36]Francis X. Clooney, "Comparative Theology," in *The Oxford Handbook of Systematic Theology*, ed. John Webster, Kathryn Tanner, and Ian Torrance (Oxford: Oxford University Press, 2007), 654. See also Clooney, *Comparative Theology: Deep Learning Across Religious Borders* (Malden, MA: Wiley-Blackwell, 2010).

[37]See the excellent review of this work from an evangelical perspective in Amos Yong, "Francis X. Clooney's Dual Religious Belonging and the Comparative Theological Enterprise: Engaging Hindu Traditions," *Dharma Deepika: A South Asian Journal of Missiological Research* 16, no. 1 (2012): 6-26.

Reading this literature, one immediately sees the potential for developing sensitivities that apply to missionary encounters. For example, as a Christian theologian, Clooney has explored the possibility of comparing two devotional treatises by Saint Francis de Sales and the Hindu mystic Sri Vedanta Desika.[38] Both writers seek a total and complete surrender to God, and so both move readers in a similar direction. The key, Clooney suggests, is not to approach these practices as an academic, interested only in the details of how they are the same or different, but rather to take the mystical goal of these writers to heart, "reading them together with a vulnerability to their power and purpose precisely so as to be doubly open to the transformations their authors intended to instigate in readers."[39] While Clooney acknowledges the tension that exists when these are read together, he wants to spend some time on that fault line, on the assumption that God already inhabits such spaces and that fresh theological insights may result from the encounter.[40]

A related conversation has been percolating in recent German theology, which has been termed "intercultural theology."[41] This discussion begins with the assumption of this book that mission must take the form of hermeneutics. That is, Christian witness is, among other things, an interpretive process in which each side becomes open and explores the proposals of the other. As these writers point out, the problem with contextualization is that it does not acknowledge "the way interpretation and contextualization are already involved from the very start."[42] This has led one theologian from this movement, Theo Sundermeier, to propose that intercultural theology is formed in the constant, and inevitable, process of what he terms "recontextualization."[43] The encounter between the missionary and the listener, Sundermeier proposes, creates a free space of multidirectional dialogue. What matters is that this allows for respecting local traditions, on the

[38]Francis X. Clooney, *Beyond Compare: St. Francis de Sales and Sri Vedanta Desika on Loving Surrender to God* (Washington, DC: Georgetown University Press, 2008).
[39]Ibid., 27.
[40]Ibid., 29.
[41]Since most of this conversation has not been translated, probably the best introduction in English is David W. Congdon, "Toward a Dialectical Intercultural Hermeneutic," in *The Mission of Demythologizing: Rudolf Bultmann's Dialectical Theology* (Minneapolis: Fortress, 2015), esp. 504-38.
[42]Ibid., 508.
[43]Theo Sundermeier develops this in *Was ist Religion? Religionwissenshaft im theologischen Kontext; ein Studienbuch* (Gütersloh: Gütersloher Verlagshaus, 1999).

one hand, while it makes space for the liberating work of the life-giving Spirit, on the other.[44] Sundermeier's proposal insists on both the irreducible strangeness of the "other" to me, and the irreducible togetherness of both. As philosophers would say, both difference and togetherness are properly basic, and they together create what Sundermeier calls *convivencia*, a dialectical way of living together that is, he thinks, the essence of mission. Like all intense cultural exchanges, Sundermeier acknowledges this will necessitate moments of syncretism, but the result is better thought of as productive of new and creative hybridities.[45] But this is appropriate to the current situation in which cultures exist amidst global flows, with porous boundaries that are both celebrated and fought over.[46]

Another perspective on intercultural theology—growing out of the same German milieu—is offered by Klaus Hock.[47] Hock believes that the current complexities surrounding religious encounters in the diversity of cultural settings are best described by what he calls "transculturation." This involves all the processes of "othering" that occur among religious actors, including exchange, destruction, reformation, and cultural creation. The key is to understand cultural difference as a creative category, "a discursive creation with a history that can be researched as it is created by processes of 'othering.'"[48] Since culture is now recognized as an open process that is the result of multiple exchanges and confrontations, Hock wants to see transculturation as a potentially generative process that can create shared values, and new cultural alignments, by mobilizing indigenous resources.[49]

NOT YOUR GRANDFATHER'S CONTEXTUALIZATION

In the remainder of this chapter, let me try to build on some of these recent discussions and propose language that can account for the new challenges. A

---

[44]As explained by Congdon, *Mission of Demythologizing*, 537-38.

[45]Ibid., 547, 550. Sundermeier acknowledges the influence of Latin American theology in his development of *convivencia* (Spanish for "living together").

[46]A good introduction to understandings of culture that reflect these new realities is Kathryn Tanner, *Theories of Culture: A New Agenda for Theology* (Minneapolis: Fortress, 1997).

[47]A helpful introduction to his thinking in English is Klaus Hock, "Beyond the Multireligious—Transculturation and Religion Differentiation: In Search of a New Paradigm in the Academic Study of Religion, Church and Interreligious Encounter," in *Theology and the Religions: A Dialogue*, ed. Viggo Mortensen (Grand Rapids: Eerdmans, 2003), 52-62.

[48]Ibid., 56.

[49]Ibid., 58.

good place to start is with one of the best recent discussions of contextualization, one offered by Scott Moreau. Here is how he describes contextualization:

> The process whereby Christians adapt the forms, content and praxis of the Christian faith so as to communicate it to the minds and hearts of the people with other cultural backgrounds. The goal is to make the Christian faith *as a whole*—not only the message but also the means of living out of our faith in the local setting—understandable.[50]

This definition pointedly seeks to move beyond thinking simply of the verbal message and wisely includes all the means of living out the faith in new settings. But note that the dominant focus, the "goal" as he says, is to make the Christian faith "understandable" in the local setting, all within a dominant paradigm of "communication." This is not so much wrong as incomplete. Let me explain.

The attempt to broaden the focus beyond the message suggests that Moreau is sensitive to the issues I have been raising. And the attempt to consider the whole of the Christian faith is surely moving us in the right direction. But a problem remains with the implication that there is some essence, the Christian faith, even broadly understood, that must somehow be made understandable—some essence of Christianity that needs to be brought into the new setting. Clearly evangelical missiologists have given up the idea that the gospel is a cargo that must simply be moved from one place to another. Indeed, the project of contextualization came about precisely to move beyond such simplistic thinking. But they have not given up, and the whole project of contextualization has promoted, the notion that there is a single thing—call it the gospel, the Christian faith, or whatever—that must somehow be communicated and received in the local context. This particular focus often restricts the ability to see something new emerging in these places.

There are two problems here. First, because, as we have seen, this gospel has often been understood in terms of a particular version, there is an assumption—often hidden—in many evangelical discussions of contextualization that God works primarily or even solely through the "message" that is being communicated.

---

[50]Moreau, *Contextualization in World Missions*, 36, emphasis original. He is quoting here his own formulation published in 2005.

In the worst case it can imply that God has actually arrived in the luggage of the missionary. The truth, of course, as we will argue at length in the next chapter, is that God was present and working in that culture long before missionaries arrived, and the indigenous values and even the religions of these people pay important tribute to this Presence. Indeed, apart from the working of the Spirit in the hearts and minds of people, preparing them to receive the good news, no message would be truly transformative.

Second, and equally important, is the reality that there is no essence of the Christian faith that is ready to be received by the hearer—no single version of the gospel that is definitive. I will argue in a later chapter that the event of Christ, and Christ's renewing work, is not indigenous to any culture—not even to supposedly Christian cultures. In every case it has to be received as a crosscultural—indeed a countercultural—reality. But this does not make it possible for us to say in advance what will be heard as good news; this will look and feel very different in each situation. Though Jesus could tell Nicodemus that he needed to be born again, and though this makes some sense in a place like America where everyone wants a fresh start, as Ralph Winter reminded his students, it only causes confusion in India: people in India want to *stop* being born again. To a Hindu who believes in multiple reincarnations, being born again does not sound like good news. Or to take a very different example, to an old man in Nigeria who worries that the spirits may attack his children during the night, the news that Christ has conquered the spirits on the cross (Col 2:15) is very good news indeed. But this news does not resonate with a Wall Street lawyer living in a gated community in Connecticut. What counts as good news in one setting will not necessarily resonate in another; indeed, it may appear bizarre. But this difference reflects the fact that the work of God must be heard and received in terms of the logic of a given culture, even when eventually it will alter that logic in critical ways. The agency of reception is always, ultimately, local. As a result, the process of witnessing to the work of Christ is invariably multidirectional. In Theo Sundermeier's terms, a way must be found to hold together the irreducible strangeness of the other and the irreducible togetherness of both as a space for the liberating work of the Spirit.

It is this multidirectional character of Christian witness, as a *locus theologicus*, that has been frequently overlooked by discussions of contextualization. To speak of a Christian faith that must be contextualized evokes a central question: Who gets to define the Christian faith? Interestingly, Christ himself pointedly did not describe the missionary calling as communicating the Christian faith, or even the good news. He urged his disciples to "go therefore and make disciples of all nations . . . teaching them to *obey* everything that I have commanded you" (Mt 28:19-20, emphasis added). Notice how the focus is on what is to be done, not what is to be thought. In evangelical missiology, this has come to include, at a minimum, the translation, teaching, and dissemination of Scripture wherever missionaries have gone. But typically missionaries have supplied something else: their understanding of the beliefs that constitute the "Christian faith" that they have brought with them.

At this point many will worry that we are saying there is more than one gospel, more than one way to God. But this worry ignores the diversity that is already apparent in the New Testament itself, where the wonderful work of God in Christ is described in multiple ways. The good news is reconciliation with God and each other, the forgiveness of sins, deliverance from the powers of darkness, a new creation, and much more.[51] Even the story of Jesus itself was formulated in four different versions (Gospels) that reflect the differing perspectives of the authors and their intended audiences. All of these reflect in one way or another the renewing work of Jesus Christ, but what part is heard as good news depends a great deal on the cultural (and indeed the personal) situation of the hearer. But notice this: the good news that is heard is not taking some form or set of practices of the Christian faith and putting this into some other setting; rather, someone in some particular setting hears one or another scriptural claim about Christ as a word from God and responds appropriately, as the Spirit moves that unique person.

Missionaries of course have increasingly recognized the necessity of this local agency. This is all to the good. But this does not necessarily solve the problems inherent in contextualization language. In the first place, even (or especially) when the people become agents in this process, a worry remains that something might be lost or mishandled in the way Scriptures are read and interpreted. In response to such worries, we have developed new categories, like "critical contextualization," that call for "someone" to judge whether the

---

[51]For a good description of this diversity, see Joel B. Green and Mark D. Baker, *Recovering the Scandal of the Cross: The Atonement in New Testament and Contemporary Contexts*, 2nd ed. (Downers Grove, IL: InterVarsity Press, 2011).

adaptation is appropriate. Hopefully, as Paul Hiebert proposed, this critical consciousness will develop within the newly evangelized people, but more often such criticism is delivered from somewhere outside that culture. In other words, the language of contextualization carries a heavy and perhaps inescapable colonial baggage and mostly presumes that someone might know better than the people themselves how to contextualize the gospel.

Meanwhile, when people begin to read Scripture and apply it in their lives, they have little or no sense that what they are doing is contextualizing something—we will see this amply illustrated in the chapter of case studies. They are simply hearing what they believe to be the voice of God and seeking to be obedient in their setting, in the same way the rest of us seek to do this in our own ways. Of course none of us who seek to follow Christ does this perfectly, which is why we need each other for encouragement and correction, but I would argue that this process of mutual learning is better described as intercultural theology rather than as contextualization.[52]

This leads me to mention two further problems with contextualization language, problems that are interrelated and need to be addressed together. From what I have just said it is clear that the attempt to put Scripture (or the gospel or Christian practice or whatever) into a particular cultural setting implies that it must be interpreted so that it will be understood there. But interpretation, what is called hermeneutics, we know, is not a culturally neutral activity. So the question of what is being contextualized hides a deeper question: Whose hermeneutics is being employed to discover what should be contextualized? Missionaries have mostly felt that they were bringing the "simple gospel," or when they realized that this had to be interpreted, they argued that their interpretations (what may not unfairly be called their prejudices) were biblically based and therefore justified.

A single example might help clarify this problem. For a generation, Western missionaries, recognizing the need for some hermeneutical method, have sought to give their non-Western converts tools by which they can properly interpret Scripture. In general, they have followed what is called the grammatical-historical method of interpretation. This is the method, widely taught in Western Bible schools and seminaries, that seeks to discover, as nearly as

---

[52]As Moreau notes (*Contextualization in World Missions*, 36), *all* Christians live in a cultural setting and seek to incarnate Scripture and Christian faith appropriately in that setting.

possible, the original meaning of the text as it might have been heard by the original readers (or listeners). It was felt that such a reading would best communicate the intention of the author, and ultimately of the Spirit of God who inspired this author. Indeed, it was claimed that ignoring this original meaning would involve a serious evasion of the truth God intended to deliver.

This made eminent sense to those of us educated in the West; we were not giving our students our own views on the matter but simply communicating what God intended to say in a given text—the "true reading." How can this be wrong? Well, it is wrong, or at least misleading, because the entire project of discovering the "original meaning" and the "true teaching" of a given text is an artifact of the last two hundred years of Western history. This search for the original meaning, as we have come to practice it in the West, has been fatally infected with a modernist and Enlightenment ethos. According to this view, history is an objective process of discovering what actually happened (cf. Leopold von Ranke). But the diversity of cultural perspectives from which history is viewed makes such a discovery impossible.

This quest for a single correct reading can be understood as a further product of the enormous shift represented by the Reformation as this was interpreted and worked out in history. Specifically, it reflects the rise of German higher criticism, in which, Talal Asad argues, "inspiration" shifted from being an authorized reorientation of life toward a *telos*, or purpose, into a psychology of artistry. The former called for reverence, careful listening, even memorization, which resulted in the believer hearing God speak; the latter implied a collection of facts that needed to be rationally comprehended and verified.[53] This is not to say that a study of the historical context is irrelevant or unimportant; however, its value does not have the determinative role often assigned to it.

Though this rational construal of Scripture is so familiar to us as to seem inevitable, such an approach to Scripture often seems odd to students in Africa and Asia who, remember, have never experienced the Enlightenment. The bare historical understanding often makes no sense in traditional settings where people live on stories and legends, and in a world populated with spirits of many kinds. Better perhaps, for them, would be to convey Scripture in terms

---

[53]Talal Asad, *Formations of the Secular: Christianity, Islam and Modernity* (Palo Alto, CA: Stanford University Press, 2003), 37.

of stories handed down by the ancestors, where by the Holy Spirit we become grafted into the story of Jesus and into his genealogy. In other words, better to think of the reading of Scripture in spiritual rather than rational categories.

Such spiritual readings often seem strange to Western students, but this is just the point. One's point of view is deeply influenced by one's cultural (and linguistic) situation. But, as I have argued, this is not simply a problem to be solved; it is a (potential) advantage to be appropriated. Incultured readings are not only inevitable; they are to be encouraged, for they can expand our comprehension of the inexhaustible riches of Scripture. So not only is the discovery of the "one true meaning" of a text impossible; it actually impedes the ability to listen and learn from each other. Over the last generation, Western scholars have begun to recognize the limitations of the historical critical method and have begun acknowledging that Scripture is received according to the spiritual and theological orientation the reader brings to Scripture—what has come to be called the theological interpretation of Scripture.[54] This recognition of the contextual and spiritual reading of Scripture fits well with the newer proposals on offer that move beyond contextualization.[55]

I have claimed that this question of hermeneutics is closely tied to another that needs to be addressed at the same time. This interrelated issue is that of the unequal political, or power, relations in which these interpretive activities are being carried out. The dominance of Western methods of interpretation reflects these unequal power relations. Jehu Hanciles has already alerted us to a central difficulty with the modern missionary movement: the complex relationships it sustained with Western colonialism and the rise of modern capitalism (both of which in fairness it often resisted). But one of the stubborn artifacts of these relationships is the imbalance that existed between missionary and native from the very beginning. Again, this is something that seems so natural and inevitable that it is mostly not even noticed.

---

[54]For an excellent introduction and survey of this method see Joel B. Green, *Practicing Theological Interpretation* (Grand Rapids: Baker Academic, 2011). There the appropriate and more modest role of historical inquiry is also laid out.

[55]For an earlier criticism of the use of Western methods, see J. Andrew Kirk, *The Mission of Theology and Theology as Mission* (Valley Forge, PA: Trinity Press International, 1997), 9, 10. See also the helpful discussion in Shawn B. Redford, "Appropriate Hermeneutics," in Kraft, *Appropriate Christianity*, 227-53.

The earliest missionaries in the Gospels were instructed to take nothing with them on their mission and to receive the hospitality of those they visited (Mt 10:10-11)—reflecting their Lord, who came to receive the hospitality of the people of Palestine.[56] In the early church the first missionaries obviously followed this pattern, as did the first missionaries to pagans in Europe and to the people of China. But things drastically changed in the modern period when missionaries began to travel only when they were fully supported by their home churches (in the West). This resulted, as we observed previously, in an inverted hospitality, in which missionaries were the ones offering rather than receiving hospitality—and, at the same time, they were the ones becoming teachers rather than learners. One has only to review the small libraries of pastors outside the West to see the overwhelming influence of Western scholarship and its ways of interpreting Scripture and theology on younger churches. But the impoverishment goes both ways: in the same way, one can lament the absence of work by non-Western scholars in libraries of American pastors![57] The project of mutual learning among the various members of the body of Christ in both cases is obstructed.

All the problems I have described contribute in one way or another to the underlying assumption of many evangelical Christians: that true faith is a set of ideas that must be "understood" and believed in order to be a true follower of Christ. In addition, there hovers over the whole project of contextualization, as this is often practiced, the whiff of hegemony based on political and economic inequality. Again, I would not want to imply that missiologists have not understood this, or that discussions of contextualization have not come to recognize and adjust for these new realities. But I argue that it is time to acknowledge the importance that contextualization has played in the history of missions and move beyond it—to admit, as Charles Kraft put it, how far our implementation has lagged behind our conceptualization. The diverse responses to the gospel that are occurring around the world suggest that the language of contextualization, by itself, is not capable of illuminating this new situation.

---

[56]On Jesus' need to receive hospitality, see Amos Yong, *Hospitality and the Other: Pentecost, Christian Practices and the Neighbor* (Maryknoll, NY: Orbis Books, 2008).

[57]See the discussion of this imbalance in William A. Dyrness and Oscar García-Johnson, *Theology Without Borders: An Introduction to Global Conversations* (Grand Rapids: Baker Academic, 2015), esp. chap. 3.

The different proposals that we explored earlier all share a common assumption about the inevitability of interreligious exchange and the potential this holds for thinking about mission in new ways. They share an openness to cultural and religious difference, a strong sense of the presence of God in these exchanges, and the necessity of making use of such places for interpreting afresh the world-changing intervention of Jesus Christ. Notice in particular the holistic nature of these encounters, which include mutual hospitality and exchanges of various kinds, not simply the exchange of ideas. Of course they also acknowledge that these exchanges produce tensions and misunderstandings, and these too are to be accepted and evaluated. Meanwhile, underlying all these fresh encounters are transcultural flows and influences that I argue are meant to spark fresh intercultural theological reflection. This assumption provides the starting point for the framework I will seek to develop in the chapters that follow.

This new situation represents a fresh opportunity for us to hear the teaching of Paul in Ephesians 4. There Paul celebrates first the (irreducible) unity that we are to enjoy in our faith and then the multiple gifts (the irreducible strangeness) that Christ has poured out on the church, gifts that are meant to build toward that unity. After noting the various ways God has gifted the people of God, Paul says explicitly that these gifts are to "equip the saints for the work of ministry, for building up the body of Christ, until all of us come to the unity of the faith and of the knowledge of the Son of God, to maturity, to the measure of the full stature of Christ" (Eph 4:12-13). This implies that maturity does not result from any single part of the body, even from the most powerful, but from all the parts together, contributing their special strengths to move toward the fullness of Christ. This further suggests to me that we need to move beyond contextualization to the celebration of the diverse places where the gospel is being interpreted and lived out, and where we can begin to learn from and correct one another in love. This also involves, so I will argue, a change of focus from the "message" that we carry with us to the presence and activity of God in these places. In the next chapter I will try to develop this theme, while in the following chapter I will move to reflect on the nature of religion and the significance of this for the new movements we are considering.

CHAPTER TWO

HOW DOES GOD WORK IN CREATION AND CULTURE?

A Theological Proposal

My first chapter, which reviewed briefly the development of contextualization, led me to suggest that the focus in missions should be less on what missionaries or pastors are doing and more on what God is doing. This observation does not result from an abundance of piety; it simply acknowledges that what we humans do is always a response to and interaction with what God is doing. Though modern persons in the West imagine they possess a certain autonomy of action—that they are the masters of their fate—this is an illusion. And while most modern persons, whether believers or not, live as functional atheists, this too reflects a misconception. Faithful discipleship is not simply about our believing certain things about God, though it includes this. It is also—and primarily—about our hearing and responding appropriately to what God is doing and saying. Simply put, discipleship is what the biblical narrative calls obedience, which is, Christians believe, a theological practice—that is, something enabled by the grace of God.

This chapter seeks to briefly develop this understanding of God's presence and work and to suggest the implications of this for our reflection on new and emergent forms of church and mission.

GOD CREATES AND SUSTAINS THE HEAVENS AND THE EARTH

One of the primary themes of this discussion of insider and emergent movements will be the centrality of the person and work of Christ, particularly the events associated with the good news—Christ's life, death, and resurrection and the gift of the Holy Spirit. But in this chapter I want to argue that the news that Christ brought belongs to a larger story that goes back to the beginning of God's creation, and that moves toward the future God is bringing about. The early chapters of Genesis state emphatically that the earth and the heavens and all that is in them exist because of the work and loving creativity of God. To return to our theme of hospitality, one way of thinking about creation is to see God as the original host carefully arranging things so that creation becomes a welcoming place both for the creatures that live there and, especially, for the human creation that is to tend and care for this divine household. The earth is home not only to humans but also to the animals and plants; even the sun and moon are neighbors and friends. It is clear from later Scriptures that, even after the tragic events of Genesis 3, God has a continuing interest, indeed a continuing presence, within the created order, working in it to show and realize divine purposes. In the expansive words of Psalm 19, the psalmist declares:

> The heavens are telling the glory of God;
>> and the firmament proclaims his handiwork.
> Day to day pours forth speech,
>> and night to night declares knowledge.
> There is no speech, nor are there words;
>> their voice is not heard;
> yet their voice goes out through all the earth,
>> and their words to the end of the world. (Ps 19:1-4)

In a striking anticipation of contemporary semiotic reflection, the psalmist notes that even human language is dependent on God-created structures. In later verses of this psalm, the writer notes how the law, which God gave to Israel, draws on and elaborates this creational wisdom: it is greatly to be desired and sweeter than honey; it revives the soul.

This continuing activity of God is evident both in a general sense—God makes the rain to fall, adorns the lily, cares for the birds, and takes delight in the creatures of the sea—and in a particular sense as God calls Abraham, delivers Israel from bondage in Egypt, and brings them into the good land (again, as a secure place the Host has prepared as a home for Israel). But God can also punish evil when he wreaks destruction on Egypt and sends Israel into exile.

Let me stress in particular two aspects of this continuing work of God in the First Testament. First, notice that the emphasis is on the *acts* of God:

creating, speaking, sustaining, delivering, and judging. Indeed, God often self-identifies as this active deliverer. As he reminds Moses in the prelude to the Ten Commandments, "I am the LORD your God, who brought you out of the land of Egypt, out of the house of slavery" (Ex 20:2). This God is not simply someone who imparts information, or makes demands, but is the final creative ground and agent in all that is. Even God's speech is integrated into the continuing creative (and re-creative) presence. This is not always easy for educated people in the West to remember. As a part of the focus on belief and reasoning that is so characteristic of the modern period, Western-educated Christians have sometimes focused more on the words than on the acts of God—more on God's attributes than on divine work.[1] As we will see, this influences not only how we view our relationship with God but also how we conceive of religion in general, and of other religions in particular.[2]

This is important because of the second aspect of God's continuing activity in creation: its purpose and goal. God's primary work throughout Scripture is the renewal and restoration of creation. Creation from the start has a particular direction. As a part of this renewing work God calls Israel to be a light to the nations and a means of extending God's blessing to all people and through all the earth (Gen 12:1-3; Is 42:1, 6; 49:6). And for Israel, renewal came to mean also deliverance from slavery: the ongoing creative work of God had to take on what theologians calls a "redemptive" character. Israel's sin and the violence of the created order had to be taken on and borne by God. Already in the First Testament the cross is foreshadowed.

God's involvement with Israel had implications also for the created order: forming Israel was a (new) creative act; it was at the same time an act of liberation. Descriptions of God's work with Israel commonly employ creation language. When Miriam celebrates God's deliverance from the Egyptians in Exodus 15, she uses the language of creation:

At the blast of your nostrils the waters piled up,
the floods stood up in a heap;
the deeps congealed in the heart of the sea. (Ex 15:8)

---

[1]For a helpful description of this problem in modern theology, see Colin E. Gunton, *Act and Being: Towards a Theology of the Divine Attributes* (Grand Rapids: Eerdmans, 2002).

[2]A detailed reflection on the nature of religion follows in chapter 5; here we intend simply the cultic and devotional practices in traditional societies by which people seek to respond to God or the gods.

And after having delivered Israel, God "planted them on the mountain" (Ex 15:17). Israel is God's creation, and, as God's special people, they are to participate with God in the healing of the earth. As God explains to Abram, "in you all the families of the earth shall be blessed" (Gen 12:3). Even the priest and temple are to reiterate the beauty of creation—the priest as the new Adam arrayed in his original splendor and the temple as a restored place of beauty and worship, a new Eden.[3]

Later, the prophets will portray Israel's unfaithfulness as an undoing of creation, in language that is unmistakably creational. Hosea laments the faithlessness of God's people, who have no loyalty:

> Bloodshed follows bloodshed.
> Therefore the land mourns,
>   and all who live in it languish;
> together with the wild animals
>   and the birds of the air,
>   even the fish of the sea are perishing. (Hos 4:2-3)

The listing of the creatures in the opposite order from the creation account underlines the fact that creation is being undone. Meanwhile, God's purposes were best captured in the great Hebrew notion of shalom, or peace, aptly described by artist Makoto Fujimura "not as the absence of war but the wholeness of humanity. It is the sense of something being renewed moment by moment."[4] Finally, the future promised by the prophets is pictured as a renewal and restoration of creation. In Isaiah's vision God announces:

> I am about to create new heavens
>   and a new earth . . .
> I am about to create Jerusalem as a joy,
>   and its people as a delight. (Is 65:17-18)

This theme of God's continuing creative work has enormous relevance for our response to the troubling and violent events unfolding today. No matter how difficult the geopolitical situation and the shifting alliances in the First Testament

---

[3]See Meredith G. Kline, *Images of the Spirit* (Grand Rapids: Baker Books, 1980), who develops this theme of the priest and temple.

[4]Interview with Makoto Fujimura, in James Romaine, *Objects of Grace: Conversations on Creativity and Faith* (Baltimore: Square Halo Books, 2002), 169.

period, God retained the initiative. And no matter how unfaithful Israel became, God did not give up on them. God says in Hosea:

How can I give you up, Ephraim? . . .
I will not execute my fierce anger;
    I will not again destroy Ephraim;
for I am God and no mortal,
    the Holy One in your midst,
    and I will not come in wrath. (Hos 11:8-9)

THE HUMAN CALL IS TO REFLECT AND WORK ALONGSIDE GOD

The human identity, and Israel's identity, is bound up from the very beginning with its call to reflect God and work with God in ordering the creation. There is an important paradox here. On the one hand, the man and the woman have their own unique roles to play. They are to work alongside God in ordering and making sense of creation. God clearly gives both Adam and Eve a role in having dominion over all the creatures of the land, sky, and sea (Gen 1:26), and in Genesis 2 whatever the "man" calls each of the animals, that is its name—God does not second guess or (directly) intervene in this ordering process. So the man and woman have their work cut out for them; as we will see, their calling is to make something of this creation, to create culture.

But at the same time, on the other side of this paradox, this culture-making work is always done *coram Deo*, that is, before the face of God. Though given work to do, there is never a sense that humans are on their own in taking care of creation. God has a continuing stake in all that happens, and the man and woman are continuously responsible to this God—a fact that Adam and Eve tragically lost sight of in Genesis 3, and that Israel would persistently forget.

In the garden, Adam and Eve's relationship to God was natural and intimate. There was no need for what we call religion, or for particular religious activity; that would not come until after the break that Adam and Eve's disobedience caused. Living before the face of God was as normal as breathing; indeed, it was a kind of dance that involved the whole of creation. As scholars have pointed out, the language of Genesis 2:15 involving God's instructions for caring for the earth—Adam is to serve and to keep the garden—is liturgical language.[5] Adam and Eve were radically with God, even as they tended the earth; this *was* their worship. As Karl Barth famously noted, it was only after Genesis 3, outside the garden, that religion, what he calls the "fulcrum of sin," enters the picture.[6] It was the serpent that suggested that the intimacy might be a mask, that God might be thought of as separate from creation, now here, now there. As Matthew Boulton puts this, "The world is thus construed as a place where merely human activity—*leitourgia*—is possible, where man and woman may live and labor on their own, beside and apart from God."[7] This of course is pure illusion, but it is an illusion that religion seeks to address and overcome.

CHRIST CONTINUES GOD'S RENEWING WORK

If God's primary work is creating and renewing, then it is possible—and in the biblical narrative necessary—to see Christ as the fulfillment of this primary work. In his teaching, in his miracles of calming the sea and feeding the multitude, in his many healings, and even in raising the dead, Christ shows himself to be the agent of God's creative work—what Christ calls the kingdom, which was now, in his person, among them. As he announces at the beginning of his ministry, "Now is the time! Here comes God's kingdom! Change your hearts and lives, and trust this good news" (Mk 1:15 CEB).

It is important that we hold together both the redemptive (or liberative) and re-creative sides to Christ's work, that is, that we understand the multidimensional character of God's work. First, as we have seen in the First Testament, God had not only to create a home for his people but also to deliver them from evil and the bondage that resulted. So Christ—both in his ministry and on the cross—had to bring about a decisive victory over the powers of evil, what Christ refers to in the parable as "tying up the strong man" (Mt 12:29). When Christ had cured the demoniac, the Pharisees were quick to see his power as demonic. But he assures them that "if it is by the Spirit of God that I cast out demons, then the kingdom of God has come to you" (Mt 12:28). This dimension will become important in our discussion of other faiths where

[5]See Matthew Myer Boulton, *God Against Religion: Rethinking Christian Theology Through Worship* (Grand Rapids: Eerdmans, 2008), 67, 68. And see Ellen F. Davis, *Scripture, Culture and Agriculture: An Agrarian Reading of the Bible* (Cambridge: Cambridge University Press, 2009).
[6]Karl Barth, *Epistle to the Romans* (New York: Oxford University Press, 1933), 240-47.
[7]Boulton, *God Against Religion*, 75.

spiritual bondage is possible. We will note there that Christ's presence represents a spiritual power superior to all competing powers. But the full narrative
of Jesus shows that this power is always in the service of the renewing and
re-creative work that makes up God's larger kingdom goals.

On the other hand, Christ came to bring life to people, an abundant kind
of life (Jn 10:10). This involved a fundamental reordering of the created order,
which represented nothing less than the inauguration of what Paul will call a
new creation (2 Cor 5:17), though the sky darkens and the earth shakes at the
death of Christ on the cross—where creational imagery reappears, representing the struggle with the powers. The cross and resurrection represent
fundamental victory over the powers of evil (see Col 2:15). The resurrection
further marks the beginning of what the prophets saw as the renewal of all
things, even as it deals with (redeems) the brokenness of the created order.
This re-creative activity continues and is manifested in the pouring out of the
Holy Spirit in Acts 2, which Peter says marks the beginning of the last days
that Joel had foreseen those many years ago (see Joel 2:28-29).

"In the last days it will be, God declares,
  that I will pour out my Spirit upon all flesh,
    and your sons and your daughters shall prophesy,
  and your young men shall see visions,
    and your old men shall dream dreams." (Acts 2:17)

So if we are to understand what God is up to in creation and re-creation,
we need to hold together this primary work of renewal and the special call
to the human creation to work together with God in this restoration as this
is enabled by Christ and the Spirit. Thus, the model I am proposing is not
the traditional one of creation–fall–redemption, the U-shaped tragedy that
reflects John Milton as often as it reflects the Bible, but rather creation–
disobedience–re-creation, with a new opportunity for all the nations to obey
God's summons. The work of Christ was not simply providing forgiveness
for sin, solving the human spiritual condition, though it surely did this. I
would claim emphatically that something new was emerging in Christ's work
that brought the whole created order to a new place where the goods of
culture (and religion) are given fresh valuation. In Christ, Paul says, we don't
look at things by "human standards"; rather, "if anyone is in Christ, that

person is part of the new creation. The old things have gone away, and look, new things have arrived!" (2 Cor 5:16-17 CEB).

Does such a model of theology ignore the terrible sin that Adam and Eve committed and the subsequent damage this caused? By no means, but it does remove it from a place at the center of the story, where it has too often resided. From the time of Augustine, theologians have argued that evil is parasitic on the good creation; it is not something substantial with its own separate reality. As Augustine taught, evil is a privation of the good of creation. Sin disorders, evil perverts—they are serious enemies—but these do not have a separate program of their own. They nip at the heel of Eve's descendants, but the Descendant has fatally struck the head of these evil powers (Gen 3:15). And the work of Christ on the cross is that definitive blow against the evil powers and the disruption caused by Adam's sin.

CULTURE AND HUMAN STEWARDSHIP

Comprehension of humanity's role in creation prepares us to understand the theological significance of human culture, and eventually of the religions that lie at the heart of every culture.[8] As I noted above, humans were given a wide assignment to take care of creation and order it—to name it and discover its significance. I want to focus for a bit on this calling because it is central to the argument of this book.

As we saw in the preceding chapter, one of the significant advances in the previous century was to discover and study the multiple cultural situations around the world. This exploration opened the way for the whole development of what has been called "contextualization." In order to propagate their faith, Christians faced the problem of how to deal with the vast multiplicity of cultures, and how the gospel was to be heard and obeyed in these various places. This led to the models developed by Stephen B. Bevans and Robert J. Schreiter, among others.[9] They carefully explored the way the Christian message may be translated into a culture, worked out by that culture,

---

[8]Note that, as I will explain in more detail, separating culture from religion, for most people and throughout most of history, would have been impossible. Even the notion of religion as a separate sphere of human activity, as we saw in the previous chapter, is a modern invention.

[9]Stephen B. Bevans, *Models of Contextual Theology*, 2nd ed. (Maryknoll, NY: Orbis Books, 2002); and Robert J. Schreiter, *Constructing Local Theologies* (Maryknoll, NY: Orbis Books, 1985).

or adapted by the culture. Helpful as these discussions have been,[10] I think for this time in the history of interreligious encounters such models seek to answer the wrong question. The question now is not how we go about placing the gospel in the culture, but rather, how do we respond, in the light of Scripture, to what God is already doing in a given culture? And how does this continuing work cast fresh light on how *we* are to understand and obey Scripture?

To elaborate this claim, or this set of claims, I need to briefly explore the importance of culture theologically (and biblically).[11] That is, I want to ask, what is *God's* interest in the various cultures of the world? *Culture* in the sense that I will use it here is all that we humans make of God's good creation. That is, cultural activity, in the first place, has always to do with all that God has made and sustains. Recall the responsibility given to Adam to name the animals, to order and give structure to what God had made, an activity in which Adam was given a free hand. Culture is always and everywhere a human project; it is what humans make of creation. Humans are not God's puppets in the creation of culture; it is their work and their responsibility, in which they exercise the freedom of the children of God. At least that was God's intent. We hear sometimes the claim that "God is globalizing the world," but this is misleading. Globalization is not God's doing; it is our doing. At the same time God is everywhere active in such cultural processes, upholding the order of things, sustaining its processes, and seeking, wooing, and calling by the Spirit those who will worship him.

Ultimately all culture making has to do with the materials and structures of creation. Of course traditions of culture embody many strands of accumulated practices and values so that much of what is at hand represents what previous generations, and even neighboring cultures, have made out of creation. But remember the other side of our paradox: though humans are responsible agents in forming culture, God has an *interest* in the process. It is God's creation after all, and it was made and continues to exist to express the glory of God. So it is not as though God begins to take an interest in human activity

---

[10]In the past I have sought to enter this debate myself. See William A. Dyrness, *Learning About Theology from the Third World* (Grand Rapids: Zondervan, 1990), chap. 1.

[11]This will be a brief exploration of themes I have developed more fully elsewhere; see William A. Dyrness, *The Earth Is God's: A Theology of American Culture* (Maryknoll, NY: Orbis Books, 1997) and *Poetic Theology: God and the Poetics of Everyday Life* (Grand Rapids: Eerdmans, 2010).

when someone begins to pray, or form and practice some religion. No, God has been intimately involved in cultural processes from the start. This means that culture making is deeply and inescapably theological. And this also assumes that the wisdom of culture often reflects the goodness, or at least the potential for goodness, of the underlying created order. Because of the structures God made and upholds, and because of the continuing work of the Holy Spirit, humans can always make something good—even, I believe, out of bad situations (just as God is busy bringing good out of evil). Further, each culture develops its own special cultural logic that makes sense of the world for those who live in that place. In the biblical material this human struggle to make sense of life and learn how to get along is featured in what is called the wisdom literature of the First Testament—Job, Proverbs, Ecclesiastes, Song of Solomon, and many parts of the Psalms and Prophets.[12]

The created order is deeply marred by human disobedience; thus, culture reflects the violence and injustice evident throughout history, from the human sacrifices of Israel's neighbors to the genocides of the last century to Boko Haram and Islamic terrorists today. This is why God's activity had to take on a restorative aspect—something often missed in calling it redemptive. But this does not keep cultures from, at the same time, developing varieties of wisdom that bring glory to God. People are always making something out of the situation they find themselves in, and often this brings about good in a way God approves. Ponder the way humans have developed the ability to grow food and domesticate animals or to discover healing remedies in certain plants. These are all things that, Scripture says, God delights in, even seems eager to take credit for.

Consider Isaiah's description of agricultural wisdom in Isaiah 28. In the context of God's promise that he is "laying in Zion a foundation stone" (Is 28:16) to establish a standard of justice opposing Israel's "covenant with death" (Is 28:18), which results in destruction, God demands Israel's attention ("listen"—reiterated four times in Is 28:23):

> Do those who plow for sowing plow continually?
> Do they continually open and harrow their ground?

---

[12]One of the best recent introductions to this material, which has been helpful to me in what follows, is Craig G. Bartholomew and Ryan P. O'Dowd, *Old Testament Wisdom Literature: A Theological Introduction* (Downers Grove, IL: InterVarsity Press, 2011).

When they have leveled its surface,
> do they not scatter dill, sow cummin,
and plant wheat in rows . . . ?
For they are well instructed;
> *their God teaches them*. (Is 28:24-26, emphasis added)

God teaches them? Yes. And when these herbs are harvested, when the grain is crushed and made into bread,

This also comes from the LORD of hosts;
> he is wonderful in counsel
> and excellent in wisdom. (Is 28:29)

But weren't these things learned and passed down from parents and grand-parents? Of course, but God apparently took special interest in this wisdom, and, in God's mind, this wisdom was integrally connected to the righteousness that God willed to bring about in the created order, and that Israel too often resisted (see Is 28:17-22).

This is the reason that God can ratify the wisdom that Israel borrows from Egypt and from Babylon—even endorsing the incorporation of sections of Egyptian literature into Proverbs.[13] *All that contributes to human flourishing, indeed everything that brings delight to the human community, God too celebrates.* Remember, God promises to "create Jerusalem as a joy, / and its people as a delight" (Is 65:18). But more than this, God has embraced this wisdom and incorporated it into the work of renewal that the First Testament recounts. God endorses this human wisdom as working toward the same goal as the redemptive interventions that make up the backbone of the First Testament narrative.

This narrative structure reminds us that the wisdom Israel borrowed is placed in a new context, within the special covenant God made with Israel. This is why Proverbs insists that "the fear of the LORD" is the beginning of wisdom (Prov 1:7), which implies that appropriate recognition and response to God is fundamental to human flourishing. But it also implies that in living a wise, or righteous, life—respecting elders, raising children, learning the way crops grow, or administering justice—one must answer to God, and God will be the final judge of what is to be approved.

---

[13]Proverbs 22:17–23:11 contains a long section taken over from the Egyptian *Wisdom of Amenemope*. Cf. J. D. Ray, "Egyptian Wisdom Literature," in *Wisdom in Ancient Israel*, ed. John Day, Robert P. Gordon, and H. G. M. Williamson (Cambridge: Cambridge University Press, 1995), 17-29.

Notice the significance of this connection between cultural practice and God's purposes. It allows us to appreciate the gifts of culture—to use them as the starting point and framework for any expression of the gospel. At the same time, this understanding of the connection offers a perspective that is able to critique those gifts. Take the common practice of gift giving, which expresses notions of obligation and reciprocity found in many cultures. Terry Muck and Frances Adeney have used this common cultural practice as a starting point for rethinking the Christian mission, something I comment on in a later chapter.[14] Just as First Testament practices were embraced in and reframed by the covenant framework of Israel, gift giving can be incorporated into and re-ordered by the gospel. Giving and receiving, in God's program, extends beyond family and tribe, eliciting practices of exchange that foreshadow a new form of human relationships, eventually entailing the reconciliation of all things.

But this connection of religious faith and wise living has a deeper impli-cation that I want to draw out. This deep connection between faith and wisdom implies that a significant part of every culture, one might say its heart and core, involves the religious practices that have developed in that place. The perennial human search for God animates culture. Religious practices reflect the human desire to respond to the gods or the powers that humans encounter, and in this desire they are also responding to the call of the biblical God. But note the implications of this: if it is true that religious traditions reflect a re-sponse, however incomplete (or even misguided), to God's call, they must be in some way capable of being included in God's project of renewing and re-storing the earth.

Evidence for this lies in the fact that Israel's religious practices, like cultural practices, were not, in the first instance, unique in the ancient Near East. Priests, sacrifices, and sacred spots were common to Israel and her neighbors. It is true that the law God gave to Moses, laid out in Exodus through Deuteronomy, includes details of religious practices—such as food preparation and appro-priate sacrifices—along with ethical precepts. God had a clear interest in all of this and demanded a specific obedience on the part of his people. But when one examines these practices carefully, even the ethical instructions (enshrined for example in the Ten Commandments), one finds that these frequently reflect

[14]Terry C. Muck and Frances S. Adeney, *Christianity Encountering World Religions: The Practice of Mission in the Twenty-first Century* (Grand Rapids: Baker Academic, 2009), 365.

widely shared practices and values in the ancient Near East. In the next chapter I will develop this point in more detail and examine its implications.

So religions must always be seen in terms of the cultures they indwell—the historical and social situations in which they have developed. As culture itself is an accumulation of human efforts and the resulting wisdom, creating spaces for medicine, science, art, and literature to flourish, so religion represents an accumulated wisdom about living in the world and endowing life with significance. Here is where the Reformation heritage that I described in the first chapter becomes a distinct handicap. Those of us in the evangelical tradition are often told that since religion is merely the human attempt to reach out to God while the gospel represents God's merciful gift to us in Jesus Christ, these various religions are all barriers to hearing the gospel. And we are further reminded that since religion animates culture, all the world's religions (except of course Christianity) have so infiltrated and corrupted their cultures that nothing short of a complete uprooting and transformation of these religions— and these cultures—will be satisfactory. Though in a later chapter I will discuss this assumption in more detail, here I want to signal the danger of such blanket assessments. Just as the various cultures have contributed their own special gifts to the human community (no culture has a monopoly on life-giving discoveries), so religions in those places often provide life-giving perspectives to people[15] and, indeed, have often been the impetus for human creativity and advancement. They have not only grounded human identity and community life for many; they have often left a residue of material and spiritual culture that we can celebrate—temples, music, dance, paintings, even legal and political practices. Moreover, like other cultural processes, religions are not static entities but are constantly evolving in response to changing circumstances; they are capable of reform and renewal as well as decay and desiccation. Indeed, I will go further and say that within each religion there is an ongoing struggle between the forces of evil and elements working for good (we will see concrete examples of this in the chapter on case studies). Recognizing this does nothing of course to deny the violence and oppression that have been perpetrated in the name of religion.[16] Unfortunately this is true of

---

[15]I distinguish life-giving properties of religions from any salvific capacity. See the discussion of this point in William A. Dyrness, *Senses of Devotion: Interfaith Aesthetics in Buddhist and Muslim Communities* (Eugene, OR: Cascade, 2013), 100-102.

[16]Karen Armstrong's remarkable new book *Fields of Blood: Religion and the History of Violence* (New

the religion called Christianity no less than of other religions. But all of this suggests that religion *in and of itself* is not the means of the renewing work that God intends to complete and has begun in Christ.

I have emphasized that the work of Christ is seen in the biblical narrative as a kind of climax of the First Testament narrative of God's work of creation and renewal, and I want to return to this point in concluding this chapter. The right-making work that God performed, and that God's people are to reflect, is seen most clearly in the right-making work of Christ. As I have noted, this is seen in his teaching and miracles (which are always to be understood together), especially as this reaches its culmination in the reordering brought about by his death and resurrection. And the presence of the Holy Spirit, the other "Advocate" that Jesus promised in John's Gospel, gives to the church and the created order more generally the dynamic necessary to continue to realize all that Jesus began to do and to teach. It is the Spirit that works in human cultures (and religions) to move people to call Jesus Lord (1 Cor 12:3).

But there is a further dimension of this New Testament fulfillment of the prophets' vision of a new creation that is important to understand. That is, Christ's work, continued in the Spirit, is not only a fulfillment of the First Testament narrative; it is also a beginning—the inauguration, as biblical scholars like to say—of the events of the end of history. Paul insists the resurrection of Jesus from the dead is the "first fruits" of the final resurrection of all things (1 Cor 15:23). This resurrection, N. T. Wright has insisted, is the sign that God intends not just a spiritual future kingdom but a renewal and re-creation—a resurrection of this order of things.[17] This means the earth, and its culture, will one day share in the renewing work of Christ's resurrection. Indeed, twice in John's vision of the new heaven and new earth in Revelation 21, he notes that the goods of cultural wisdom will be celebrated in the new creation. In his description of this New Jerusalem, John says that kings of the earth "will bring their glory into it" (Rev 21:24), and a few verses later John sees that the people will "bring into it the glory and the honor of the nations" (Rev 21:26). According to Scripture, this is the final goal of history.

York: Knopf, 2014), however, disputes the common assumption that religion is the primary cause of human violence.

[17]See N. T. Wright, *Surprised by Hope: Rethinking Heaven, the Resurrection, and the Mission of the Church* (New York: HarperOne, 2008).

This chapter has argued that God's primary work is to be the loving creator. Because of human disobedience, however, this creative work had to take on a redemptive or salvific character. The creator had also to become in Christ the Savior. But these goals, creation and redemption, are not to be separated from one another; they both constitute aspects of the unified work of God in creation and history. Let me be clear that I have not intended in this chapter to present a coherent account of all that Christians have believed and taught; I have sought rather to describe, according to Scripture, the basic situation in which we find ourselves: God is busy restoring creation so that it fulfills his original creative purposes. If this is true, then clearly God continues to work in all the cultures of the world and in all the cultural wisdom that one encounters there—in all the structures and efforts that promote human flourishing. But insofar as the religions of these places promote (or oppose) such flourishing, God also takes a personal interest. As God said to Cain in Genesis 4: "If you do the right thing, won't you be accepted? But if you don't do the right thing, sin will be waiting at the door ready to strike! It will entice you, but you must rule over it" (Gen 4:7 CEB).

So what guidance can we distill from these reflections for our project of assessing God's presence and work in insider and emergent movements? Three possible emphases come to mind.

First, it is clear that God is at work reordering a fallen world, and therefore all efforts that contribute to this end will elicit God's approval. Just as God was eager to take credit for cultural advances in the First Testament, it is likely that similar advances today will reflect the ongoing work of God's Spirit moving all things toward the new heaven and new earth. This complete renewal will not happen until Christ returns to complete what he has begun, but this promised future provides a quality and a direction toward which God intends creation to move. God takes delight both in the cultural renewal of human ingenuity and in the renewing work of the Spirit. Where the one leaves off and the other begins is often a mystery we cannot decipher. But we can be confident that where movements celebrate and further such a renewal in righteousness, God is surely at work.

Second, just as God delights in goodness and new signs of life, so those responding to this, and all the gifts of creation, with thanks and praise must be pleasing to God. Prior to the dark description of human sin that Paul offers

NO

in Romans 1, he points to a fundamental attitude of indifference and ingratitude as a crucial precondition for sinful behavior. Although God's power and divine nature are plainly visible for all to see, people do not properly acknowledge this. "For though they knew God, they did not honor him as God or give thanks to him." And because of this failing, Paul goes on, they "became futile in their thinking, and their senseless minds were darkened" (Rom 1:21). Social disorder and ingratitude were born together, as the Genesis account makes clear. But those movements and places where people are inspired to offer God thanks and praise must contain an impulse that God approves.

Third, the biblical narrative is also clear that this ongoing work of the Spirit, and whatever cultural renewal might be evident, should finally draw people to see in Jesus Christ—and eventually in his death and resurrection—the focus and center of God's renewing purposes. A properly trinitarian understanding of God's purposes suggests that the broader working of the Spirit will lead people, eventually, to come see these purposes realized in Christ. The renewing work of the Spirit is an application of the transformation God brought about in the death and resurrection of Christ. People may not at first see all these connections and draw out all the proper implications. But a fundamental movement in this direction, an openness to the centrality of Jesus and a longing for God's renewing work, will surely be characteristic of movements we ought to celebrate.

But here is my larger claim: if God is present and working in this or that situation by the Spirit, addressing people in what theologians have called prevenient grace or the general call, this address must be framed in the terms and logic of that culture. This means that we have to pay particular attention to both the logic and the structure of a culture, but also to the ways this logic comes to expression in the religions of that place. This means further that the renewal that God intends will be a regeneration of *that* logic and structure. Frequently in the missiological literature one sees reference to some "Christian" truth that lies hidden within a given culture. For example, some have sought to see Hebraic images (of, say, a sacrificial lamb) embedded in Chinese characters, or claimed that the Japanese people constitute a lost tribe of Israel because of the similarities between the ark of the covenant and the *omikoshi* (the portable Shinto shrine carried in festivals). Or, more commonly, some have sought out "redemptive analogies" in a given culture where they claim the

Christian gospel has been foreshadowed.[18] But, quite apart from whether these quests are justified on historical or linguistic grounds, such efforts risk reducing the religious core of these cultures to a previously constructed (and mostly Western) version of the gospel. Further, this may keep us from seeing how God might be working in unique ways within other cultures and thus blind us to fresh illumination of the renewing work of God in Christ.[19]

I have made some references to biblical materials in this chapter, but we still need to explore more fully the treatment of religion and culture in Scripture. How biblical materials might shape our attitudes and responses to these cultures and their religions is the subject of the next chapter.

---

[18]The best known of these is probably Don Richardson, *Peace Child*, 4th ed. (Ventura, CA: Regal Books, 2005).

[19]I am grateful to Daniel Reid for recalling this tendency in the literature and for suggesting examples.

CHAPTER THREE

RELIGION IN THE BIBLICAL NARRATIVE

I n the first chapter I argued that the inescapable religious pluralism of the early twenty-first century has offered a new challenge to mission that the dominant conversations about contextualization fail to adequately confront. In the second chapter I attempted to construct a brief theological framework structured by a narrative of God's creative and redemptive work in Israel and in Christ. This narrative, in the scriptural account, took its shape in particular cultural and religious settings, which it reflects and at times resists. The reflection and resistance are the subject of the present chapter.

FIRST TESTAMENT ATTITUDES TOWARD RELIGION

Let me begin with a brief review of the general understanding of religion that emerges in the First Testament. The varying attitudes toward religion in the First Testament reflect both the religious and the cultural environment that Israel inhabited and also what God was up to at a given time. Early in Israel's history their religious practices appeared indistinguishable from those of their neighbors. For some time now, scholars have recognized that Canaanites had sacred sites where they offered sacrifices, and Israel adopted these sites and this practice. Helmer Ringgren noted a generation ago that Gilgal, Bethel, and Shiloh, among other cultic sites, were most likely taken over from the Canaanites. Ringgren observes: "The sacredness of the spot is simply taken for granted; the Canaanites sacrificed there, and the immigrating Israelites simply took over these cultic sites from the Canaanites."[1]

---

[1]Helmer Ringgren, *Israelite Religion*, trans. David E. Green (Philadelphia: Fortress, 1966), 49.

The text of Genesis recounts the patriarchs' use of such sites without any sense that these could not be appropriately used for the worship of Yahweh. At the beginning of her history at least, Israel had a sense that the God who had called Abraham could be worshiped through the forms inherited from the existing religious environment. Indeed, this was the only approach to God available to them.

Abraham's encounter with Melchizedek provides a striking example of this influence. In Genesis 14, Abraham (then called Abram) has to rescue his nephew Lot, who has been taken captive by four kings. After the victory of his small army, Abram/Abraham is met by another king, Melchizedek, who is also called a "priest of God Most High" ('ēl 'elyôn). The text notes that Melchizedek blessed Abram and said:

"Blessed be Abram by God Most High,
    maker of heaven and earth;
and blessed be God Most High,
    who has delivered your enemies into your hand!"

And Abram gave him one-tenth of everything. (Gen 14:19-20)

Scholarship on this meeting has often tried to make Melchizedek into a "hidden Israelite believer" when, in fact, as Robert Johnston has recently argued, the text clearly indicates that "the conduit for God's blessing here is a foreign priest acting in the integrity of his own beliefs."[2] Moreover, Abram's encounter with Melchizedek (lit. "king of righteousness") was a further revelation to him of the one supreme God whose character reflects justice and righteousness. So important is this person that his role is praised in the book of Hebrews as "resembling the Son of God, [remaining] a priest forever" (Heb 7:3). Thus Christ's own high priestly role is described as resembling Melchizedek's—becoming a priest not through legal requirements (that is, through a particular religious structure) but "through the power of an indestructible life" (Heb 7:16). Clearly God's larger purpose, reflected in this episode, is not to institute some particular religious practice but to bring about an order characterized by righteousness that will issue in the blessing of all.

---

[2]Robert K. Johnston, *God's Wider Presence: Reconsidering General Revelation* (Grand Rapids: Baker Academic, 2014), 92. The debate over the meaning of this passage is summarized in pp. 91-94.

God does later give Moses, in the books of Exodus and Leviticus, explicit instructions about cultic practices, as well as detailed ethical guidelines. But even these were not entirely unique to Israel. As we noted in the last chapter, even the moral guidelines canonized in the Ten Commandments, for the most part, represented a widely shared moral consensus—something that surfaces in the narratives of the book of Genesis. This, at least initially, appears troubling to many students of the First Testament. What are we to make of the similarities with the religions of Israel's neighbors?

In the twentieth century, under the influence of Karl Barth and the biblical theology movement, biblical scholars tended to emphasize the distinctive character of Israel's religion over against the paganism of the surrounding culture. But as more archaeological material came to light, the parallels with neighboring religions became harder to ignore. Scholars have generally recognized the parallels while at the same time warning against making too much of them.[3] The general consensus is reflected in Thorkild Jacobsen's conclusion that Israel's religion, as this is developed in the Scripture, "opened up possibilities that may have been incipient in Mesopotamian religion but did not develop out of it."[4]

Patrick Miller's survey of Israelite religion provides a helpful summary of First Testament teaching and practice. The relationship between Israel and her neighbors, he thinks, represents "an ongoing process of appropriation and transformation of aspects of the divine world and culture ordering as they were manifest in Israel's environment." Rather than borrowing, Miller thinks a better image is that of inheritance. "Israel," he argues, "taking form as a community of faith, inherited religious elements from the world in which it came into being." The uniqueness of Israel's faith, he concludes, belonged to the particular God that Israel worshiped, not necessarily the special forms that worship took. Indeed, forms of worship that originated in the surrounding cultures, as we have shown, were often incorporated into God's own instructions to Israel.[5]

John Goldingay, however, thinks that there is more to be said about Israel's relationship to her neighbors. With respect to the religions of Israel's neighbors,

---

[3]One has to distinguish between the modern archaeological discovery of parallels and the teaching of Scripture about such things. It is the latter that we seek to discover.

[4]Cited in Patrick D. Miller, *Israelite Religion and Biblical Theology* (Sheffield: Sheffield Academic Press, 2000), 143.

[5]Ibid., 154.

he writes: "It is possible to recognize foreign religions as reflecting truth about God from which Israel itself may be able to learn." This we saw clearly in the case of Melchizedek's blessing of Abraham. Goldingay goes on to say, though, that these religions themselves were "always in need of the illumination that can only come from knowing what God has done with Israel."[6] These religions, Goldingay believes, should be seen as sources of illumination and not simply expressions of lostness. It is well known that the Hebrew 'Ēl and its cognates derived from the Canaanite name for the head god of the pantheon, and this name was also used in Genesis to refer to the God of Abraham, Isaac, and Jacob (see Gen 14:19-22). At the same time, what God was doing with these patriarchs was important also for the Canaanites themselves precisely because of the way God's work with Israel would critique Canaanite religion. Indeed, what was happening in Israel would have significance for all people because it was to become part of the story of Jesus Christ.

This appropriation of an existing name for God has many parallels in the history of the Christian church and continues to be debated right up to the present—as we will see in a later chapter. Patrick Miller points out that, though the God of Israel was what ultimately made Israelite religion unique, at the earliest stage of Israelite history this God appears as a typical Late Bronze or Iron Age god, an image that would change as God's relationship with Israel developed.[7] In the First Testament there seems to be a variety of appropriate responses to the gods of Israel's neighbors, ranging from acceptance, as in the Canaanite 'Ēl, to rejection, as in the worship of Baal during the time of Elijah and as seen in the book of Hosea.

On the evidence provided by these scholars, we might offer some general conclusions. With significant exceptions, God shows a remarkable tolerance toward other religions in the First Testament. In a passage where God forbids Israel from making idols, God says, "When you look up to the heavens and see the sun, the moon, and the stars, all the host of heaven, do not be led astray and bow down to them and serve them, things that the LORD your God has allotted to all the peoples everywhere under heaven" (Deut 4:19). Has God

---

[6]John Goldingay, "How Does the First Testament Look at Other Religions?," in *Key Questions About Christian Faith: Old Testament Answers* (Grand Rapids: Baker Books, 2010), 248.
[7]Miller, *Israelite Religion*, 154.

allowed then this kind of false worship, as a kind of "interim acceptance"?[8] Deuteronomy 32:8 similarly suggests this:

> When the Most High apportioned the nations,
>> when he divided humankind,
> he fixed the boundaries of the peoples
>> according to the number of the gods.

However, both passages go on to emphasize that it will not be so with Israel; God brought them out of Egypt to be a special and treasured people who would worship only Yahweh.

But there are clear exceptions to God's tolerance, if that is what it was. God is opposed to the prophets of Baal and sacrifices offered in support of their supposed power. But, interestingly, when God does express anger at other religions, it is not for cultic impropriety but for moral reasons. Elijah opposed the prophets of Baal (in 1 Kings 18) because they had caused Israel to sin. Though Israel could worship Yahweh under the name of *ʾĒl*, they could not do the same with Baal (see Num 25:3-5). But here again the problems were not cultic but moral. Worship of Baal, perhaps as a fertility god, was associated with sexual impurity. In one of the most extensive treatments of Israel's flirtation with Baal worship, the eighth-century BCE prophet Hosea condemns Israel for seeking in the Baal cult the continued fertility of the earth. The second chapter of Hosea makes the point that fertility is not guaranteed by the cult (not even by Israel's cult practices!). Only the creator God delivers fertility to the earth—Yahweh is the true fertility God. This fruitfulness is guaranteed by God's covenant promises, to which cultic worship is meant only to be a grateful response.[9]

But note that in Hosea, God's judgment is also delivered against Israel, not because of wrong cultic practices but because of violations of the moral demands of this God. The Lord has a dispute with his people, Hosea announces:

> There is no faithfulness or loyalty,
>> and no knowledge of God in the land.

---

[8]This is Goldingay's suggestion, that this worship may have been in some way allowed by God. See Goldingay, "How Does the First Testament," 253-54.

[9]See William A. Dyrness, "Environmental Ethics and the Covenant of Hosea 2," in *Studies in Old Testament Theology*, ed. Robert L. Hubbard, Robert K. Johnston, and Robert P. Meye (Waco, TX: Word, 1992), 65-70.

GOD'S DAMNATION OF IDOL WORSHIPPERS IS *NOT* TOLERANCE. ALSO NOT MORAL (BUT THE LAW)

Swearing, lying, and murder,
> and stealing and adultery break out;
> bloodshed follows bloodshed.
Therefore the land mourns,
> and all who live in it languish. (Hos 4:1-3)

Similarly, when God turns attention to the neighboring religions, it is not primarily their cult practices that are condemned. In the table of nations and religions in Amos 1–2, God speaks against their violence, their inhumanity—what we would today call war crimes—not against their religious practices. As Nicholas Wolterstorff argues, God "declares that 'evil' will befall them on account of such behavior, this evil being 'sent' . . . by the Lord. What Amos assumes is that they knew better, or should have known better."[10] There was a universal understanding of morality to which God held them accountable.

Interestingly, in Amos it is only when God addresses Judah that religious practices come in for critique. But even there it is their rejection of Torah (Amos 2:4), their crushing of the weak, and their turning away the poor (Amos 5:11-12) that spark God's wrath. Their moral insensitivity is so problematic that, in the face of rampant injustice, God can no longer tolerate their burnt offerings and gifts of food (Amos 5:21-22):

Even though you offer me your burnt offerings and grain offerings,
> I will not accept them;
and the offerings of well-being of your fatted animals
> I will not look upon. . . .
But let justice roll down like waters,
> and righteousness like an ever-flowing stream. (Amos 5:22, 24)

Though Israel's religious practices were not always unique to Israel, as with other areas of cultural wisdom, they were placed in a special covenant setting, within the narrative of God's work that would lead to Jesus Christ, and thus their cult practices carried a higher level of responsibility to this God. Their corporate life was to embody the special covenant relationship with God and reflect in some special way the character of this God, and the special renewing work God had undertaken.

---

[10]Nicholas Wolterstorff, *Justice: Rights and Wrongs* (Princeton, NJ: Princeton University Press, 2008), 84.

We might put matters this way: religion in the First Testament was to be taken up into God's renewing work in creation; it was to serve and further that work. And this demanded that particular moral sensitivities were to be embodied in the social structure and even in their agricultural practices—sensitivities and practices that were unique to Israel. With regard to social structure, the Torah stipulated a communal order that paid special attention to those who, for various reasons, were marginalized by the dominant power relations: the widow and orphan were cared for, and the poor were allowed special privileges in the harvest. As with religious practices, the social patterns of Israel in themselves were not unique, but the way these were to be shaped was to uniquely reflect God's renewing work. For example, slavery was common in the ancient Near East and was also practiced in Israel. But in the regulations placed on slave holding there is this remarkable instruction:

> Slaves who have escaped to you from their owners shall not be given back to them. They shall reside with you, in your midst, in any place they choose in any one of your towns, wherever they please; you shall not oppress them. (Deut 23:15-16)

Escaped slaves were not to be returned to their owners, on the assumption that they escaped because of abuse or some other just cause. Indeed, they were free to live wherever they liked! In nineteenth-century America, not returning slaves was a capital offense; apparently slave owners who defended slave owning from the Bible had not read it very carefully.

Similarly, the First Testament recognizes the need to offer collateral for a loan. But while recognizing the legitimate claims of such economic arrangements, the instructions proceed to subvert these when they conflict with the claims of justice. So if your neighbor offers his coat as collateral and is poor, "you are not allowed to sleep in their pawned coat. Instead, be certain to give the pawned coat back by sunset so they can sleep in their own coat" (Deut 24:12-13 CEB). This practice then would offer an opportunity for them to see what kind of God Israel serves, for whom moral claims trump economic ones. This passage concludes: "They will bless you, and you will be considered righteous before the LORD your God" (Deut 24:13 CEB). God's ears are specially tuned to the needs of the poor; Israel is not to take advantage of them. Their salary is to be paid "the same day, before the sun sets, because they are poor, and their very life depends on that pay." Why? Because they will cry out "to the LORD. That would make you guilty" (Deut 24:15 CEB). Just wages and working conditions are matters of special concern to God.

Similar principles are expressed with respect to creation care. Israel's responsibility to care for creation was to reflect the fact that God, as the creator, is the ultimate owner of the land, and therefore no human ownership was to be permanent. (Absolute ownership of private property in the Western tradition was introduced by means of Roman law.) This of course would have huge repercussions for how any law would be administered even if it did not, in itself, imply any specific policy on land ownership. The sabbath principle, which called for land from time to time to lie fallow, provides a basic metaphor for stewardship of the land. The instructions make clear this is for the sake of the Lord: "In the seventh year there shall be a sabbath of complete rest for the land, a sabbath for the LORD: you shall not sow your field or prune your vineyard" (Lev 25:4). The Jubilee or fiftieth year, a kind of sabbath of sabbaths, similarly specified that land that had been "bought" should be returned to the original owner, and everyone should "proclaim liberty throughout the land to all its inhabitants" (Lev 25:10). Such instructions signaled that God was the final owner, who demanded justice. These practices provided structural adjustments that were intended to assure the fair distribution of the goods of creation. That Israel was often unfaithful to these covenant stipulations does not diminish the importance that God placed on just social and economic arrangements.

As became clear in the Prophets, God was primarily interested not in religious practices in themselves, not even those stipulated in the Law, but in how those practices served the larger interests of God's renewing and justice-making work. As we have seen, God was critical of Israel's religious practices precisely when they no longer promoted righteousness. Recall God's anger in Amos 5:

> I hate, I despise your festivals,
>> and I take no delight in your solemn assemblies. . . .
> But let justice roll down like waters,
>> and righteousness like an ever-flowing stream. (Amos 5:21, 24)

When Micah asks whether he should bring the offerings to the Lord that the Law commanded, he is reminded:

[God] has told you, O mortal, what is good;
    and what does the Lord require of you
but to do justice, and to love kindness,
    and to walk humbly with your God? (Mic 6:8)

If God did not demand religious practices that were unique and unlike others of that time, then clearly it was not Israel's religion in itself that assured them of God's favor. What then was Israel's special significance? John Goldingay puts the matter this way: Israel's significance lay in the people's status as *witnesses* to the living, saving God—to the things God has done. As he summarizes this point, "The gospel is good news, not a good idea. It states that in the history of Israel and of Jesus, God has acted in love to restore humanity to God and to its destiny. The gospel is the news that God created the world, stayed involved with it when it went wrong, became involved with Israel in order to put it right."[11] And this ultimately led to God becoming part of the created order in Jesus the Jewish rabbi, to make clear (and make possible) what it means to be human.

Perhaps we can draw out a further implication of this news that is relevant to our argument: God's purposes in Israel and in Christ make up the center of the story, but they do not define its periphery. Notice that the First Testament makes clear from the very beginning that the purposes of God were broader than those comprehended in a people who keep the law. From the call of Abraham it was clear that God intended, through Israel, to bless all the nations of the earth (Gen 12:1-3). Moreover, the heirs of Abraham—as numerous as the stars in the sky—would surely encompass other peoples alongside the seed of Jacob. One does not have to wait until the prophets in order to glimpse God's justice-making purposes; these were already evident in the special provisions of the law that we have described. God intended to form a people and a society that, in their care for one another and for the earth, would embody and reflect the renewing and redemptive work of God. It is this cosmic program that Christ came to realize—what he calls "the kingdom" and what we intend when we refer to "the gospel." While the details of this program were unavailable to followers of other religions, its concern for justice, for making things right, was often glimpsed. Wolterstorff affirms that

---

[11]Goldingay, "How Does the First Testament," 261.

while an awareness of justice is available to all nations, and more particularly an awareness of the requirements of justice for the vulnerable low ones, false religion impairs that awareness. God's Torah, issued to Israel but meant to be heard by all eventually, is a corrective. The Torah formulates in the mode of commandment the universal requirements of justice.[12]

RELIGION IN THE MINISTRY OF JESUS

We turn now to the specific implications of the New Testament and the work of Christ for our attitudes toward religion. We can see already from the narrative of Scripture that the final meaning of the events unfolding around us, all that we think of as historical events, lies within the purposes that God has for the created order, and in the end toward which it tends. The key to this lies in what we call "gospel"—that is, the events associated with the life, death, and resurrection of Jesus.

The ambiguity of First Testament attitudes toward Israel's religious practice is consistent with Jesus' attitude toward his own religious heritage. On the one hand, Jesus gave no indication that his Jewish heritage was unimportant or that it was something that should now be discarded. As I claimed in an earlier chapter, there is no indication that Jesus intended his followers to start a new religion. To the contrary, Jesus was faithful in his visits to the temple, and he appeared to observe with his disciples the major Jewish holidays. On the other hand, it became clear in the course of his life and teaching that, with his appearance, the practice of this faith was being transformed.

Consider how Jesus never hesitated to speak out against the hypocrisy of those who occupied positions of religious authority and were diligent in the details of First Testament law but failed to exercise compassion toward the needy. Jesus came into conflict with the Pharisees most often over issues of purity.[13] Purity was central for him, but he brought a distinctive emphasis to bear on the traditional interpretation. The litany of complaints in Matthew 23 (apparently delivered in the temple!) lists the many ways the Pharisees violated God's purposes even as they carefully kept the First Testament

---

[12]Wolterstorff, *Justice*, 85-86.

[13]Cf. Bruce Chilton, who said, "Jesus understood purity in a way which brought him into conflict with a straightforward, priestly interpretation of Scripture." Chilton, "Judaism," in *Dictionary of Jesus and the Gospels*, ed. Joel B. Green, Scot McKnight, and I. Howard Marshall (Downers Grove, IL: InterVarsity Press, 1992), 404.

prescriptions: "Woe to you, scribes and Pharisees, hypocrites! For you tithe mint, dill, and cummin, and have neglected the weightier matters of the law: justice and mercy and faith" (Mt 23:23). As with the First Testament prophets, Jesus' critique was moral, not religious. Or put another way, religion was to serve the justice-making work of God as seen in Jesus' ministry.

Moreover, recall how Jesus sometimes appeared to the rabbis to play fast and loose with the law in his own observance—gathering food or healing on the sabbath. Here he defended the practice by lashing out at the hypocrisy of religious leaders: "Does not each of you on the sabbath untie his ox or his donkey from the manger, and lead it away to give it water? And ought not this woman, a daughter of Abraham whom Satan bound for eighteen long years, be set free from this bondage on the sabbath day?" (Lk 13:15-16). But in all cases he insisted that his practice was consistent with First Testament teaching. As he says to the crowds of the Pharisees who sat on Moses' seat: "Do whatever they teach you and follow it; but do not do as they do" (Mt 23:3), for they are more concerned with their status than with service to the people.

Mark 7 is often proposed as a critical passage indicating Jesus' abrogation of (at least) the ceremonial aspects of First Testament law. In contrast to the Pharisees' insistence on the kosher practices of preparing and eating foods, Jesus appears to say that only what expresses the heart matters, not what one eats. Jesus says: "Do you not see that whatever goes into a person from outside cannot defile?" (Mk 7:18). After which Mark comments, "Thus he declared all foods clean" (Mk 7:19). Characteristically, Jesus goes on to emphasize the scandal of immoral practices that issue from within the human heart: fornication, theft, murder. "All these evil things come from within, and they defile a person" (Mk 7:23). But a recent study by Daniel Boyarin, a distinguished Jewish scholar, questions whether Jesus' views were so divergent from rabbinic teaching. Rather, Boyarin argues, Jesus consistently served as a conservative critic of the "traditions of the elders," pointing out ways these had obscured the original intention of the law. In this and in other cases, Boyarin argues, "the explanation that Jesus gives is to interpret the deep meaning of the Torah's rules, not to set them aside. And it is this deep interpretation of the Law that constitutes Jesus' great contribution—not an alleged rejection of the Law at all."[14]

---

[14]Daniel Boyarin, *The Jewish Gospels: The Story of the Jewish Christ* (New York: New Press, 2012), 127.

Boyarin's argument supports the view that, throughout his ministry, Jesus' attitude toward the law and Jewish religion was one of authoritative reinterpretation. Jesus summarizes this in the Sermon on the Mount: "Do not think that I have come to abolish the law or the prophets; I have come not to abolish but to fulfill" (Mt 5:17). When he saw the temple made into an arena of buying and selling, he pushed over the tables and said: "It is written. 'My house shall be called a house of prayer'; but you are making it a den of robbers'" (Mt 21:13). Though he honored the law, in his teaching and practice the law was being reinterpreted and, in signaling the righteous kingdom that God intended to bring about, its original purpose affirmed. As he goes on to say after the passage noted above about tithing: "You tithe mint, dill, and cummin, and have neglected the weightier matters of the law: justice and mercy and faith" (Mt 23:23). In fundamental ways, as Boyarin argues, this attitude was perfectly consistent with the teaching, especially, of the First Testament prophets who sought to recover the original meaning of the Torah.

There is one further point that needs to be made about Jesus' attitudes toward religion that will be important for what follows. In sending his disciples out Jesus gave them power (authority) over the spirits and the ability to heal as they proclaimed the reign of God. They were to take nothing with them but receive the hospitality of those to whom they went. Moreover, he emphatically demanded his disciples avoid all violence in protecting either his own life—as in the case of Peter's attack in the garden (Mt 26:52, 55)—or in support of the coming kingdom. Jesus tells Pilate: "If my kingdom were from this world, my followers would be fighting to keep me from being handed over to the Jews. But as it is, my kingdom is not from here" (Jn 18:36). The gospel, in other words, is to make its way by the power of the renewing work that God was bringing about in Christ and in the subsequent gift of the Holy Spirit, not via the machinations of political or military might.

RELIGION IN THE BOOK OF ACTS AND IN PAUL

But, while his priorities are clear, Jesus' attitude toward Jewish religion is not easy to comprehend, and certainly cannot be reduced to a formula. Indeed, these ambiguities gave his enemies ample material they would use to condemn him to death. And it is safe to say that despite (or because of) Jesus' example, his disciples struggled to understand the role their Jewish religion was to play after the resurrection. Certainly the book of the Acts of the Apostles seems to take its start both literally and figuratively from the Jewish temple and the practices associated with it. But before long it became clear that things were changing. And the apostles had no special wisdom to know how the in-breaking of God in Christ was to affect the religious practices they treasured. The book of Acts is in many ways the account of their debates about this.

One of the best examples of what appeared to them to be the changing attitude of God toward people's religious practice is found in Acts 10. In that chapter Cornelius, a Gentile God-fearer who prayed faithfully and gave alms, has a vision from God and is told to summon Peter. At the time of Cornelius's vision, Peter, who cannot imagine his life as other than a faithful Jew, also has a vision in which he is asked to violate Jewish purity laws. He immediately protests, and God has to tell him, "What God has made clean, you must not call profane" (Acts 10:15).[15] In fact, to get the message across, God has to repeat the message three times (perhaps recalling Peter's threefold denial of Christ). Amidst the bewilderment that both Peter and Cornelius experience, God brings them together. In the ensuing conversation, they exchange stories of God's working in their lives with the result that the religious assumptions of both are deeply challenged.

Two elements of God's work are evident here. First, Peter has to come to realize that his Jewish faith does not constitute the limits of God's saving activity in the world. It is not as though God is saying the Jewish faith no longer has relevance to God's work. In fact Peter, in his message to Cornelius, explicitly connects the new work of God in Christ to the First Testament prophetic tradition that one would come to be the "judge of the living and the dead" (Acts 10:42). Nor is it the case that Christianity has now replaced Judaism, as is often thought. Peter's insight is more constructive and more far-reaching than this. He confesses, to his own amazement: "I truly understand that God shows no partiality, but in every nation anyone who fears him and does what is right is acceptable to him" (Acts 10:34-35). However, Peter goes on to declare that this realization is supported and not undermined by the apostolic gospel. He immediately recognizes that the realization that "God

---

[15]It is not necessary to suggest God is abdicating these purity laws here; rather, God is using the vision to suggest that no person is impure or unclean, which an overly strict reading of these laws had suggested (see Acts 10:28).

doesn't show partiality to one group of people over another" (Acts 10:34 CEB) is in fact the message, the good news, which God sent to Israel through Jesus Christ, Lord of all. "You know the message he sent to the people of Israel, preaching peace by Jesus Christ—he is Lord of all" (Acts 10:36).[16]

But this realization by Peter that God works also beyond the confines of Israel is connected to a second discovery. As Peter was speaking, he saw that the Holy Spirit fell on everyone listening. This amazed both Peter and the circumcised believers who accompanied him—to say nothing of the Jerusalem church that learned about this in the next chapters. In his defense before the troubled Jerusalem leaders, Peter testifies that when all this happened he remembered the Lord's words: "John baptized with water, but you will be baptized with the Holy Spirit" (Acts 11:16). So Peter concludes, "If then God gave them the same gift that he gave us when we believed in the Lord Jesus Christ, who was I that I could hinder God?" (Acts 11:17). Notice that what came first was the experience, the work of God; the theological interpretation followed. Peter, and eventually the early church in developing their theology, first took account of what God was doing with these new believers and then began their systematic reflection on their experience and its context in the First Testament. To their credit, they were willing to adjust their theory (i.e., their theology) to the new work of God they were observing. This unusual encounter between culturally and religiously different people represented a hermeneutical space in which both were forced to work out the meaning of the new thing God had done in Christ.

Consider next the important address of Paul in Acts 17 in Athens. Paul's strategy and teaching here also have large implications for the developing view of religion in relation to the work of Christ. Note that Paul begins by acknowledging and appreciating what was surely a rather promiscuous pattern of religious practice. (Luke comments laconically "the city was full of idols," Acts 17:16.) Paul stands in the middle of the council on Mars Hill and describes the way he has observed their religious devotion: "Athenians, I see how extremely

---

[16]This new vision is elaborated by Paul in Galatians 4:8-10. There Paul seems to equate the Jews' living under the law with the Gentiles' control by the elements of the world. Both are confronted with a "new creation." See Peter Leithart's discussion of this passage in *Delivered from the Elements of the World* (Downers Grove, IL: InterVarsity Press, 2016), 36-41. Leithart points out that Paul here "radically flattens the difference between Jew and Gentile." See the discussion of the Jerusalem council that follows in this chapter.

[Handwritten marginal note: BUT WE NOW HAVE THE SCRIPTURES]

religious you are in every way" (Acts 17:22). But then he goes on to put their religious pursuit into a larger framework: "From one ancestor he made all nations to inhabit the whole earth, and he allotted the times of their existence and the boundaries of the places where they would live, so that they would search for God and perhaps grope for him and find him" (Acts 17:26-27). Then he goes on to quote one of their own poets (Epimenides, sixth century BCE) in support of this divine presence: "In him we live and move and have our being" (Acts 17:28).

Note first that God made all the nations or, better, peoples (*ethnoi*), from a single parent—that is, all share a common ancestry. Paul, rather than promoting any religious test, begins with the simple assertion that they all share a common story. Rather than referring his listeners to the patriarchs, where his own religious narrative began, he refers them to a larger narrative that begins with creation—a narrative that he shares with his Epicurean or Stoic listeners. Whatever national or religious loyalty one feels, Paul implies, or whatever individual or family pride people may exhibit, the truth is that they all—we all—share a common humanity. And, second, God allotted times and places that these people would inhabit. The identities of these people were to be tied to and expressive of particular times and places in God's creation. And the purpose of this distribution is explicitly so that they would have opportunity to search for, and perhaps find, God—though God, he notes, is not far from any of us (quoting still another Greek poet). But now, Paul says, things have changed: God has intervened in Christ's life and resurrection in such a way that a new era of responsibility has dawned. In Christ the earth and its people are called to a new level of accountability.

Several important if tentative conclusions may be drawn from this passage. Paul expresses here (and elsewhere, as in Rom 1) the clear biblical teaching that human religious practices are to be respected because they reflect a basic truth about humanity—namely, human beings' deep need of God and their inclination to search for him. Indeed, Paul takes the religiosity of the Athenians as his starting point in presenting the gospel to them. The implication is that apart from this search for God, apart from religion, one could not expect the message of Christ to be heard. As I will note in more detail in a later chapter, this has been a theme that theologians have often developed, from Augustine's God-shaped vacuum to Calvin's sense of God, and even John

Wesley's general call. All of these recognize the created connection of humans with God or, better, their inbuilt inclination to worship and praise God. *NO*

But Paul here implies something else as well. Though the dispersion of peoples in creation had as its fundamental purpose that they would seek after God, we may not conclude from this that God simply approves of all religious practices. As we have argued, God's response to religion is not static but changes in ways that reflect various times and circumstances. This is because of the inadequacies of human religion on the one hand and the changes necessary because of the continued working of God on the other—in this case the appearance of Christ. First, we must recognize that religion, though it represents an inbuilt longing for God, is subject to human error and indeed includes an inclination to reject God and God's purposes. According to the New Testament, human responses to God's presence have at times been incomplete, as in Acts 17:23, and at other times distorted and perverse, as in Romans 1:21-23. This latter passage lays out in more detail the human tendency to worship the creature rather than the creator. But I find it interesting, as I noted in the last chapter, that while Paul describes their inclination to idolatry, he recognizes that "though they knew God, they did not honor him as God or give thanks to him" (Rom 1:21). Their religious perversion was not merely adherence to wrong religious practices; it reflected a more fundamental refusal to acknowledge and properly honor the God they knew. *AUDIENCE OF ROMANS?*

Second, God's attitude toward religion also changes because God continues to intervene and work for human salvation, particularly in the life, death, and resurrection of Jesus Christ and subsequently in the giving of the Holy Spirit. So Paul says to the Athenians, while God had previously overlooked *NO* human ignorance, because of the coming of Christ and specifically because of his death and resurrection, God "now directs everyone everywhere to change their hearts and lives" (Acts 17:30 CEB).

This is not to say that all the believers were agreed on what such a change involved, especially with respect to the religious practices existing at the time. These questions continued to trouble the waters through the first several centuries, as we will see. But in Acts things were brought to an interim resolution in what is called the Jerusalem Council described in Acts 15. The issue appeared straightforward: was it necessary for new believers in Christ, who were Gentiles, to be circumcised according to the custom of Moses in order to be saved? The "Judeans" (represented by some in the Jerusalem church) believed that it was; Paul and Barnabas thought this was unnecessary for Gentile believers. Again, the evidence presented before the council was not textual or historical but anecdotal or, better, testimonial. Paul and Barnabas "reported all that God had done with them" (Acts 15:4). A heated debate followed, and after Peter again recounted what God had done, James suggested that this may in fact be a fulfillment of First Testament prophecy that "all other peoples may seek the Lord—even all the Gentiles over whom my name has been called" (Acts 15:17). The primary evidence submitted is Peter's experience in Acts 10; the fact that the Spirit was given to Cornelius is interpreted as a sign and wonder on the level of those seen in the ministry of Christ. As R. H. Stein notes, the church did not "decide" that circumcision was no longer necessary for Gentile believers; they simply "recognized" this as following from what was obviously a work of God.[17]

The formulation they sent to the churches includes this summary of their decision:

> The Holy Spirit has led us to the decision that no burden should be placed on you other than these essentials: refuse food offered to idols, blood, the meat from strangled animals, and sexual immorality. You will do well to avoid such things. (Acts 15:28, 29 CEB)[18]

How are we to understand this decision?

Timothy Tennent argues that these stipulations represent the insistence that believers separate themselves from their previous pagan religious identity. He notes: "The prohibitions served to visibly separate the Gentiles from their former religious identity, since all four of these requirements are linked to common pagan practices of the time."[19] But this suggests it would have been possible to separate their religious and cultural identities, something a first-century person would have found difficult to do.

---

[17]R. H. Stein, "Jerusalem," in *Dictionary of Paul and His Letters*, ed. Gerald F. Hawthorne, Ralph P. Martin, and Daniel G. Reid (Downers Grove, IL: InterVarsity Press, 1993), 469.

[18]Markus Bockmuehl argues that this decision reflected a recovery of the Noachian covenant from Genesis 9. There God promises to bless the earth and gives everything for food but stipulates: "Only, you shall not eat flesh with its life, that is, its blood" (Gen 9:4). See Bockmuehl, *Jewish Law in Gentile Churches: Halakhah and the Beginning of Christian Public Ethics* (Edinburgh: T&T Clark, 2000), 162-67. I owe thanks to Cory Willson for this reference.

[19]Timothy C. Tennent, *Theology in the Context of World Christianity: How the Global Church Is Influencing the Way We Think About and Discuss Theology* (Grand Rapids: Zondervan, 2007), 204.

Markus Bockmuehl has proposed a better solution. He has found an important source for this decision in the rabbinic dialogues about the Noachian commandments (in Gen 9:3-7). In a discussion with significance for the argument of this book, Bockmuehl (quoting Rabbi Novak) notes that the Noachian commandments helped Judaism situate itself vis-à-vis the multicultural Gentile world, and over against Greco-Roman ideas like the *ius gentium*, by suggesting an international morality that made ethical communication possible. The discussion in Acts 15, based on Peter's narrative of Acts 10, assumes that Gentiles like Cornelius were already saved. The question was not one of salvation but of whether Gentile believers should be treated as proselytes or Noachians. Bockmuehl argues that the decision was not a compromise but a spelling out of implications that, as Gentiles, they could be held to the same (Noachian) ethical standards that would be applied to righteous Gentiles living among the people of Israel as resident aliens.[20] Clearly this was not intended to provide a universal religious structure but represented rather an ad hoc response to the new work of God, in the light of that particular set of circumstances. At the same time it recalled prophetic attitudes toward neighboring faiths, an adherence to a higher standard of justice that God intended to be embodied in any appropriate religious structure.

From our review of biblical perspectives on religions, we have seen that though God's work of renewal in Israel and in Christ has implications for both culture and religion, at the beginning it always accommodated itself to the religious realities on the ground. Israel's religion emerged from a combination of influences that included divine instructions and inherited patterns from the wisdom and practices of surrounding cultures. That is to say, though the gospel is God's news, it did not drop from heaven but was given by God in and through existing cultural and even religious structures—which, remember, it has always been God's purpose to transform.

In the New Testament the gospel came to the world out of the Jewish tradition, but, as with God's call to Abraham in Genesis 12, it was meant as a gift that would eventually bless all peoples. Mary's song in Luke 1 emphasizes this point:

[God's] mercy is for those who fear him
   from generation to generation.

---

[20]Bockmuehl, *Jewish Law in Gentile Churches*, 162, 164-66.

He has shown strength with his arm;

> he has scattered the proud in the thoughts of their hearts. . . .

according to the promise he made to our ancestors,

> to Abraham and to his descendants forever. (Lk 1:50-52, 55)

Christ's ministry persistently challenged the ritual boundaries the Jewish religion had established (at least in the tradition of the elders), even as he and his disciples continued in the temple and remained faithful Jews. So it is understandable, even inevitable, that initially Judaism was central to New Testament worship, now being reoriented by the death and resurrection of Christ and the gift of the Holy Spirit—the new exodus event.

As we have seen, the implications for the future of religious practice and for the believers' continuing relation to Judaism were hazy at best. As theologian Andrew Walls notes, when the apostles decided Christians did not need to become Jewish proselytes and accept circumcision, the "implications were huge . . . and no one could guess where they would lead."[21] But notice that the challenge involved all the dimensions of religion. It was more than simply a change of vocabulary; it involved sensitive cultural and religious negotiations involving belief, practice, and place. Paul described part of the dilemma when he wrote to the Corinthians: "Jews demand signs and Greeks desire wisdom" (1 Cor 1:22). That is, the one was interested in what should be done (should believers be circumcised?); the other wanted to know what is to be thought (how can God appear in human form?). Early in Christian history Paul offered a good example of the way religious traditions are inclined to talk past one another, as indeed they have done ever since.

So the initial question, which resonates with the overarching question of this book, was this: What would the Christ event mean for the future of Judaism? But belief in Christ also raised a similar question about the future of emperor worship. Both—Judaism and emperor worship—had their zealous defenders. Both traditions worried that the worship of Christ would be destructive of all they loved and valued, indeed of their very identity. But even in the New Testament it is clear that such displacement was not the necessary outcome. When the Roman worry was expressed in the question of paying

[21]Andrew F. Walls, "The Rise of Global Theologies," in *Global Theology in Evangelical Perspective: Exploring the Contextual Nature of Theology and Mission*, ed. Jeffrey P. Greenman and Gene L. Green (Downers Grove, IL: InterVarsity Press, 2012), 23.

tribute to the emperor, Christ made clear that appropriate honor could still be paid to the emperor, even if worship had to be reserved for God alone.[22] But what did it mean to render to God the things that are God's? In Mark 12 just after Christ's instructions about payment of tribute to Caesar, he warns those scribes who might be considered retainers of imperial privilege: Beware of those "who like to walk around in long robes . . . and to have the best seats in the synagogues and places of honor at banquets! *They devour widows' houses* and for the sake of appearance say long prayers" (Mk 12:38-40, emphasis added). Echoing the prophets of the First Testament, Jesus emphatically condemns religious practices that impede the pursuit of righteousness and justice and deflect the renewing work of God.

Similarly, Paul struggled to reconcile his deep Jewish identity with his newfound faith in Christ. Though he expressed his wish that his fellow Jews would come to Christ, and insisted that Christians were simply being grafted onto the stem of Israel, the precise nature of that relationship going forward was not specified. Surely the relationship needed to remain close, tethered as the two traditions were by a common dependence on the First Testament—that is to say, sharing a common story—but what social and religious form should this take? Again, the requirement that Paul proposes has to do with righteousness: they are to steadfastly pursue or seek the righteousness of God rather than their own (Rom 10:3). And when it comes to this calling, "there is no distinction between Jew and Greek; the same Lord is Lord of all and is generous to all who call on him" (Rom 10:12).

I suggest that this time and place—this clash of Jewish, Gentile, and Greco-Roman worlds—represented a particular hermeneutical space in which the events of the gospel had to be (re)interpreted and lived out. This involved pressures both from the side of Jewish orthodoxy and from the side of pagan practices the Gentiles knew, both seen in the light of their understanding of the call of the gospel. Notice that both approached matters with legitimate interests and concerns. Why in Acts 15 did they settle on these particular standards and not others? To modern eyes these provisions constitute a strange and rather minimalist list. I would offer two, closely related, reasons. First,

---

[22]Karen Armstrong points out that the Greek used for "render" to Caesar (*apodote*) "was used for a rendition made when one recognized a rightful claim." Armstrong, *Fields of Blood: Religion and the History of Violence* (New York: Knopf, 2014), 139.

these instructions addressed practices that constituted the identity of the Gentiles who had come to believe on Christ as Savior. Even if they would not be framed in this way in the future, at that time and place they were practices that were important to many believers, and for the rabbis they suggested universal standards God intended. But, second, and perhaps another way of saying the same thing, these practices and the worlds they elicited constituted part of the cultural resources that were on offer at the time—the Gentile practices and the debates among the rabbis, which had to be both seized and resisted. They were part of the cultural repertoire that those seeking to be faithful to Jesus Christ had to engage and in some way critically appropriate. As Stein argues, "the issue at stake, according to Luke, is not justification, but social intercourse between Jews and Gentiles."[23]

The larger point I am making should be clear. These religious practices were not constitutive of the saving faith the apostles were calling for, but neither were they indifferent or irrelevant to that faith. The grace of Jesus Christ had to take shape in the particular cultural patterns that prevailed at that time, while at the same time reflecting some universal standard of morality. And the final determination of that, though it involved a good deal of debate and even confusion on the part of the apostles, rested finally on their determination of what God was doing in the new situation in which they found themselves.

Looking back on the account in Acts, it is easy to imagine that the issues were clearer than they were. But we have seen the consternation these recent events caused among the Jewish believers in Christ. And it is also easy to assume, since we have the benefit of twenty centuries of hindsight, that we know precisely what God was doing and read this back into the account. But two examples from Paul's letters may remind us of the difficulties that attended the events surrounding Christ's death and resurrection. In the first, Paul returns in several places to the fraught relations that prevailed between Jews and Gentiles. What does the work of Christ mean for this? Early in the book of Galatians, one of his earlier letters, Paul had ventured a kind of summary statement: "In Christ Jesus you are all children of God through faith. As many of you as were baptized into Christ have clothed yourselves with Christ. There is no longer Jew or Greek, there is no longer slave or free, there is no longer male or female; for all of you are one in Christ Jesus" (Gal 3:26-28). But this

---

[23]Stein, "Jerusalem," 471.

summary apparently did not clarify things, for Paul had to return to the issue throughout his ministry. Is there truly no difference between Jew and Gentile? Later in Ephesians Paul attempts to work out what it means that God has planned to "gather up all things" in Christ (Eph 1:10), specifically for relations between Jews and Gentiles. In Ephesians 2 he notes that Christ had broken down the dividing wall between Jews and Gentiles, which did not mean these differences no longer mattered; rather, in Christ each has access to the other, even as each is given a higher level of responsibility for the other (Eph 2:14-16). Paul had to address over time an issue of ethnic relations that continued to agitate the developing churches and work out for these Christians the meaning of Christ's work of renewal.

In addressing a second contentious issue in the brief letter to Philemon, Paul considers the question of what Christ's work means for slavery, so critical in a world where slaves constituted a majority of the population. Apparently Onesimus is a runaway slave, and perhaps even a thief, whom Paul has won back to the gospel and who has been serving the apostle during his captivity in Rome. Paul decides to send Onesimus back to Philemon, who is an elder and a leader in the church that meets in his home. But Paul urges Philemon to accept Onesimus, not simply as a servant (slave) but even as a brother, which he has become to Paul. "Perhaps this is the reason he was separated from you for a while," Paul notes, "so that you might have him back forever, no longer as a slave but more than a slave, a beloved brother" (Philem 15-16). Paul emphasizes "a beloved brother—especially to me but how much more to you, both in the flesh and in the Lord" (Philem 16).

In these verses we see the extraordinary power of the gospel to change lives, and even social institutions. But as is evidenced in the sad subsequent history of gender and race relations, this was not something accomplished once for all but a challenge that believers have had to face in every generation. The cultural and religious implications of this were anything but clear then, and they are not always clear even for us these many generations later.

CONCLUSION

Though we have more ground to cover, let me attempt a provisional summary of this chapter. From the biblical narrative we might conclude that though religion can be a carrier of authentic faith and the means of offering appropriate thanks and praise to God, God does not take delight in religion in and of itself. John Goldingay's comment is apropos: "There is salvation in no religion because religions do not save. Not even Israel's religion saved them. It was at best a response to Yahweh, the living God who had saved them. And only this God can save."[24] Religion in itself cannot offer salvation for the simple reason that God, not religion, is the source of salvation. Religion can be a witness to this God and this salvation, but it can also be an obstacle, even in the case of the special privilege accorded to followers of the Jewish faith. Paul reminds the Christians in Rome, who might have been tempted to claim some imperial privilege, that there is a special place given to Israel: "To them belong the adoption, the glory, the covenants, the giving of the law, the worship, and the promises; to them belong the patriarchs, and from them, according to the flesh, comes the Messiah" (Rom 9:4-5).

But it was not altogether clear to Paul, as it is not at all clear to readers of this chapter today, what this would mean for the Jewish religion going forward. The reason, as Paul goes on immediately to remind readers, is that God alone is the source of salvation and not religious practice: "the Messiah, who is over all, God blessed forever. Amen" (Rom 9:5). Paul is at pains to stress that God had a special role for Israel to play and that this role was not abdicated with the coming of Christ. And though Jewish religious practices in themselves did not constitute the fullness of God's provision for human salvation, they provided critical and indispensible hermeneutical spaces that allowed believers to work out the meaning and implications of Christ's life and work.

These religious practices represented resources and situations in which people were called to responsibility before the living God. And I will argue that other religions *mutatis mutandis* may offer their own spaces in which people can seek after God.[25] Of course they can no doubt represent the futility of human attempts to reach God, but might they not also represent potential places where Christ can be encountered and God's project worked out? Might they be spaces where something is set in motion, a fresh impulse of the Spirit? This possibility can be illustrated using specific case studies, and it is to these we now turn.

[24]Goldingay, "How Does the First Testament," 244-45.
[25]The Jewish religion as the means of God's provision of a Messiah of course stands in a different relation to followers of Christ than to followers of other religions. But as we have seen, this difference cannot be taken to mean God takes no interest in these other spaces.

CHAPTER FOUR

CASE STUDIES OF INSIDER MOVEMENTS TODAY

U p to this point our conversation has proceeded at a high level of generality. As I mentioned in the first chapter, this is perhaps a necessary response to a situation in which many of the movements we might be interested in are, in various ways, inaccessible to the researcher. But in a globalized and inter-connected world this situation is rapidly changing, and in this chapter I will examine several important cases that have achieved some visibility (though even here, in some cases, the geographical details and names have been changed). These will be largely drawn from Asia for reasons I will set out. But first I will turn to some historical examples from Latin America and Africa.

Examining particular cases immediately forces one to consider additional political and sociocultural realities that more general inquiries tend to overlook. Two we hinted at earlier are worth considering again here: the post-colonial situation and the shifting, contentious realities of globalization. In a recent comparative study of Hindu and Christian devotion, Michelle Voss Roberts has recognized the fraught character of the Western Christian's attempts to engage other religions, a worry that is particularly relevant to the examination of insider movements. She observes: "Christian knowledge of the world's religious traditions is inevitably embroiled in the colonial impulse to appropriate, consume, exploit, and market other cultures." She proposes that Christian scholars must therefore approach neighbors of other traditions "in a spirit of friendship chastened by a history of Christian hegemony."[1] As

---

[1]Michelle Voss Roberts, *Tastes of the Divine: Hindu and Christian Theologies of Emotion* (New York: Fordham University Press, 2014), xx. Her observations address the special relationship between Christianity and colonialism that we described in chap. 1.

we will see, this history not only carries implications for the researcher's attitudes, but, even more importantly for this study, it has invariably influenced how newly formed non-Western believers in Christ construe their relation to the (largely Western and colonially tainted) Christian tradition.

A second, related concern is the frequently contentious, and often violent, relationships that prevail among religious traditions today, especially in Asia, though because of global interaction, increasingly evident elsewhere as well. In fact, it is safe to say that the primary visible encounter between religions today, at least as this is reported in mainstream media, is one of violence and conflict. This raises the question of whether appreciative and thoughtful pursuit of new forms of relationship, under these circumstances, is even appropriate. If this contentious relationship were determinative, books like this might be considered not only unnecessary but perhaps counterproductive for those in dangerous situations.

Two brief responses may be made to this second concern. First, we must be careful not to let mainstream media, and the attitudes and reactions suggested there, limit our Christian reflection and response to the current interreligious climate. The truth is that millions of people, most especially in Asia, live in peaceful relations with neighbors of other faiths, indeed in extended families of mixed faiths, and have done so for generations. It is in such situations that the movements that we study have arisen. But, second, even if it were true that violence has too often become normal among people of different faiths, Christians who are called by their Lord to live at peace with all people and to love and pray for their enemies should never capitulate to this situation as though it were inevitable or unchangeable. Rather, they should be busy preparing themselves for the day in which people from every tribe and nation will praise God in their own manner and in their own language. This hope is enough to justify the reflections represented in this study.

HISTORICAL SOUNDINGS IN INTERFAITH AND EMERGENT MOVEMENTS: LATIN AMERICA AND AFRICA

Before turning to contemporary Asian cases, I want to make use of two case studies from other parts of the world that might illuminate, and thus mitigate, the postcolonial handicap to which I have referred. These examples come from the precolonial and colonial history of Latin America and the modern colonial period of Kenya, in East Africa. These examples drawn from the history of Christian missions are an altogether appropriate reminder that emergent movements have been characteristic of Christian outreach throughout its history. They are an important starting point for a further reason. I have argued in the second chapter that our starting point is not the communication of the Christian message across borders but the awareness of God's presence and working in all of history and in all the nations of the world. This living Presence becomes particularly salient in the following examples. Like many insider movements today, they have to do not with the communication of the Christian message but with the clear presence and working of God, and the various responses to this, especially as this was illumined by fresh reading of Scripture.

a. Latin America. Reflection on the long precolonial and colonial history of Latin America has come in for increasing study in the last generation. We have already noted the critical study of Willie James Jennings and the detrimental influence that period has had on the development of Western theology.[2] Here I want to turn to an important study by Costa Rican theologian Elsa Tamez on the (similarly overlooked) role of indigenous religious traditions in the forming of Latin American religious identity.[3] Tamez begins with the assumption, which I share, that the revelation of God did not begin with the arrival of the Spaniards. Rather, since God is present and active in all cultures, there must have been an awareness of God's presence in precolonial Latin America, or more particular to her concern, in Mesoamerica. She says "our interest ... [is] to demonstrate that the revelation of God goes far beyond our Christian circle, for God's grace extends to the totality of creation, in its different times and different places."[4] Her article is an attempt to explore and assess in particular the precolonial experience of God in the light of the coming of Christianity.

Tamez proceeds to explore the precolonial Náhuatl culture centered in what is now Mexico and describes the original belief in the god Quetzalcóatl,

---

[2]See Willie James Jennings, *The Christian Imagination: Theology and the Origins of Race* (New Haven, CT: Yale University Press, 2010), and the literature cited there. See also William A. Dyrness and Oscar García-Johnson, *Theology Without Borders: An Introduction to Global Conversations* (Grand Rapids: Baker Academic, 2015), chap. 1, for a further survey of literature on this region.

[3]See Elsa Tamez, "Reliving Our Histories: Racial and Cultural Revelations of God," in *New Vision for the Americas: Religious Engagement and Social Transformation*, ed. David Batstone (Minneapolis: Augsburg Fortress, 1994), 33-56, and the literature cited there.

[4]Ibid., 36.

which in the Náhuatl language means "feathered serpent."[5] In Náhuatl mythology Quetzalcóatl represents the god of life who injures self to bring a new humanity (a fifth creation) into existence. Tamez describes this account:

> The core of this story relates how the God Quetzalcóatl struggles against the lord of death and his reign so that a new humanity might rise into existence; the struggle is taken to such an extent that Quetzalcóatl injures Self in order to give humanity life.[6]

As they recounted these stories, and as they were enacted in various ritual forms, the Náhuatl became acutely aware that their very lives were dependent on the self-sacrifice of Quetzalcóatl. This god was always remembered with deep affection and, after the time of the conquest, with nostalgia. For sadly during the fifteenth and sixteenth century (in the period coinciding with the Spanish conquest), this benign theocracy was replaced by a military dictatorship, and the warrior god Huitzilopochtli supplanted Quetzalcóatl, who was moved back into the thirteenth heaven, the place reserved for the "old gods of generations past."[7] Though Huitzilopochtli, the warrior god of the Aztecs, was quick to claim the power associated with the earlier search for internal purity and mystical union, his warrior emphasis on violence represented what Tamez calls a "perversion of religion." Huitzilopochtli had testified:

> My principal coming and my work is war. . . . I have to gather and maintain the lot of every nation . . . but I do not do so graciously. . . . From the four corners of the earth you have to conquer, win over, and enslave others for yourselves. . . . You likewise have to pay with your sweat, work and pure blood.[8]

Though this dark period included practices of brutality and even human sacrifice, a spirituality of repentance and forgiveness associated with the ancient religion and the god Quetzalcóatl was always kept alive.[9]

This was the struggle taking place in Náhuatl religion when the conquistadors arrived in Latin America. Tamez argues that a similar sedition had

---

[5]"Feather" is a symbol for the heavenly realm, and "serpent" is a symbol of the earthly realm, so this "feathered serpent" represents an interesting representation of an incarnational form—ascending and descending. Ibid., 36.

[6]Ibid., 37.

[7]Ibid., 40.

[8]Ibid.

[9]Ibid., 41, 42.

already taken place in the god the Spaniards brought with them. Instead of the God who brought life and liberation in Christ, the Europeans brought a God who needed to conquer others. Hernán Cortés sadly echoed the words of Huitzilopochtli when he wrote in his memoirs: "But our Lord wanted to show his great power and compassion to us, for despite all our weakness we broke their pride and arrogance, and many of them died." This included the slaughter of six thousand unnamed people by Pedro de Alvarado in the high temple during the feast of Tóxcatl, along with many other atrocities. It did not take the natives long to realize that this "Spanish" God was even more violent—and more potent—than Huitzilopochtli. "In essence," Tamez concludes, "there was no difference between the reigning God of the Aztec empire and the God of the Spanish empire; they both subdued and murdered."[10]

Indeed, Tamez points out, the parallels between these religious traditions were remarkable. In both religions there was an active, ongoing "struggle of the gods," and this struggle, she thinks, should be conceived of not as a struggle between Christianity and the native faith but rather as a struggle within Christianity itself—one that mirrored the battle within the Náhuatl tradition.[11]

Just as there were those in traditional Mexican cultures who refused to honor Huitzilopochtli the warrior god, soon after the conquest there arose Christians who opposed the enslavement and exploitation of the indigenous people. The Dominican Fray Antonio de Montecinos claimed the "voice of Christ" and declared: "I have risen up here to be the voice of Christ in the desert, which is this island. . . . That voice says that you are in mortal sin, and therein will you live and die, for the cruelty and tyranny that you have used against these innocent people. Are they not human beings?"[12] Though his superiors disputed his views and returned him to Spain, his appeal—echoing the biblical call of justice and equality—was soon taken up by others, most notably the Bishop of Chiapas, Fray Bartolomé de las Casas.[13] De las Casas saw that because of the actions of the Spanish, the Christian God was being demeaned. He wrote:

---

[10]Ibid., 43-44.
[11]Ibid., 47.
[12]Ibid., 49-50.
[13]See the important study of de las Casas by Gustavo Gutiérrez, *Las Casas: In Search of the Poor of Jesus Christ* (Maryknoll, NY: Orbis Books, 1993).

> The Indians do not take from anyone what is not theirs, nor do they injure others, nor bother them . . . and they see Christians committing every type of crime and evil; . . . finally they ridicule and mock what is taught them about God but that which some of them do not believe, to the extent of mockery, [*sic*] is not what is truly esteemed by God, they see God as the most iniquitous and evil of God, based on the example of those who worship that God.[14]

The resulting "conversion" of the continent resulted more from the military might of the Spanish than from any power of the Christian gospel; this victory was nothing more than a surface "Christianization." In the end, Tamez avers, one religious system was imposed in place of another.

After this comparison of religious conflicts, Tamez asks the obvious question: Why could the Christian vision that came to Latin America not "tolerate the existence of other living faiths, even when they might contain features similar to the gospel?"[15] Of course it is understandable that Huitzilo-pochtli would be rejected, but why was Quetzalcóatl also regularly demonized, unless this attitude reflected a consistent belief that all indigenous faiths are barbaric and diabolical? Happily, the story in Latin America did not end with this impasse. Not only were there missionaries, like de Montecinos and de las Casas, who more truly represented the good news that Christ brought, but before long something interesting and momentous began to happen. Little by little indigenous testimonies emerged that the God of the Bible was in fact the same as that honored in their own ancient traditions. In the so-called dialogue of the twelve, indigenous voices recognized the same attributes in the biblical God as in their own ancient god, and one of them affirmed: "We will worship their God, because I have discerned that their God is the same as ours."[16] But in the Náhuatl culture an even further step was taken that speaks directly to the argument of this book. That is, not only did Náhuatl culture accept the Christian God,

> but it includes that God as part of its own indigenous vision of the cosmos. That integration is taken to such an extent that there is a live, religious continuity between the God of life and the Christian God, which comes together under the figure of the indigenous virgin of Guadalupe.[17]

[14]Quoted in Tamez, "Reliving Our Histories," 50.
[15]Tamez, "Reliving Our Histories," 52.
[16]Ibid., 54.
[17]Ibid., 55.

True conversion in this sense did not necessitate abandoning their own spiritual heritage—something that would have been tantamount to denying their own identity. Rather, it meant reimagining this heritage in the light of the new situation; the further revelation of Christ was giving new life to the ancient faith, making possible a renewal of that faith from within. As Paul demonstrated on Mars Hill, their reflection on the gospel could be funded in part by their own religious experience, even if that experience would eventually be transformed by the encounter with Christ.

The centuries-long encounter between Christianity and the native traditions did not represent a simple power encounter between the gospel and unbelief. It was rather a unique hermeneutical situation that gave fresh opportunity to work out the meaning of the Christian story, and the work of Christ in a new place. While Protestants may not find the Virgin of Guadalupe a life-giving symbol, for many Latino Catholics she represents the integration of parts of themselves that they could not bring together in other ways. For remember it was a Náhuatl boy, Juan Diego, to whom the Virgin first appeared in the original sixteenth-century account of this apparition. But reflecting on this encounter, and its subsequent history, provides even outsiders an opportunity to see something about Christ's coming that they did not see before. Indeed, the mutual learning offers an excellent example of intercultural theology. As Tamez concludes, through this "the Spirit of Christ as well as the Spirit of Quezalcóatl are evangelizing us."[18]

This impelling account puts in a whole new light the crucial question, do we worship the same God? And this is something we will explore in the next chapter. Alongside the question of whether Christians and Náhuatl worship the same God, one might just as reasonably ask whether Hernán Cortés and Antonio de Montecinos, despite their common religious heritage, were worshiping the same god! Notice too the way the people's identity, tied as it was to their religious heritage, quite naturally determined what they took away from the missionary intervention. And this proved, in the long run, to be an asset rather than a liability; they were not blind to the fact that the message of Christ had been fatally contaminated by the military and political might that accompanied the missionary presence. But on the other hand it was this same

---

[18]Ibid., 56.

heritage that gave them containers that made it possible for them to comprehend the "news" about Christ—to correct and fill out their own religious life. And as they learned from Christ, we have learned from them, even if this mutual learning was neither immediate nor widespread. Indeed, it represents an emergent and contested process that continues even to this day.

b. Kenya, East Africa. From the older colonial encounter in Latin America, we turn to the twentieth-century colonial experience of the Gikuyu people in what is now Kenya. East Africa, a British protectorate since the nineteenth century, formally became a crown colony in 1920, a situation that continued until Kenya gained its independence in 1963. Under colonial administration the missionaries from Britain and America were welcomed, though indigenous movements representing various indigenous faiths—a perennial presence in Africa—often existed in uneasy relations with the foreign missionary presence.[19]

The conflicts between local Kenyan interests and the colonial and missionary presence came to a head in the 1920s.[20] The missionary appeal was to the individual African and assumed that conversion involved a radical break from his or her social past. Jomo Kenyatta, the first president of Kenya, described this period:

> The early teachers of the Christian religion in Africa did not take into account the difference between the individualistic aspects embodied in Christian religion, and the communal life of the African regulated by customs and traditions handed down from generation to generation.[21]

Though Africans during this time were also experiencing the heavy hand of the colonial administration, conflict with the traditional mission churches was

---

[19]The classic study of these movements is David B. Barrett, *Schism and Renewal in Africa: An Analysis of Six Thousand Religious Movements* (New York: Oxford University Press, 1968).

[20]See on this movement and its development, Francis Kimani Githieya, *The Freedom of the Spirit: African Indigenous Churches in Kenya* (Atlanta: Scholars Press, 1997), 33-39. Githieya, an Akorino leader, first prepared this manuscript as a PhD dissertation at Emory University. This discussion of Kenya is also indebted to an unpublished paper: "Akorino Church: A Reading of Theology from an African Indigenous Church in Conversation with Kwame Bediako and Immanuel Katongole," by Jacob Kimathi Samuel, who is currently conducting research on the Akorino Church for a PhD dissertation at Africa International University, Nairobi, Kenya.

[21]Jomo Kenyatta, *Facing Mount Kenya* (1938; repr., Nairobi: Heinemann Kenya, 1978), 270-71. Notice the assumption Kenyatta makes that Christianity is intrinsically individualistic, something I have been disputing in this book.

more disruptive. The missionaries generally opposed traditional practices—
the dances, female circumcision, polygamy, and even male initiation ceremonies, most of which they did not understand and frequently misinter-
preted.[22] They appropriated large tracts of land for their commercial
agriculture and perceived the Africans as ready labor for their projects. All of
this contributed to the breakdown of traditional family patterns and, not surprisingly, sparked protests (which were often led by young converts educated
in the mission schools).[23]

Sometime in 1926 Joseph Ng'ang'a, in a drunken stupor, had a dramatic
encounter during which he heard God's voice giving him a new name and
vocation that he later interpreted as an experience of baptism of the Holy
Spirit. The voice told him that God had seen the sufferings of his people under
the British and that he, Joseph, would help bring about their liberation.[24] Another leader, Musa Thuo, had a similar vision, and these leaders came together
to form the Akorino Church (also called the *Arathi*, lit. "prophets" or "those
who see visions"), founded as an independent Christian movement.[25] These
leaders sought to follow closely the biblical instructions—from both the Old
and the New Testaments—which led them to reject not only the practices of
witchcraft and sorcery but also Western ways of dressing and eating. They
became known for their flowing white robes and turbans (still visible on the
streets of Nairobi today) and their insistence that healing was to be a gift of
the Holy Spirit, not a result of Western medicine.

Significantly, despite the contemporary struggles with the mission churches,
the Akorino Church did not begin as a breakaway movement from any
Christian denomination but sprang directly from the experiences of these prophetic figures who felt a divine calling to this ministry.[26] While there were
many factors at play in the rise and popularity of the movement, scholars are
agreed that it was the publication of the New Testament in the Gikuyu language in 1926 that ignited the revival that gave rise to the Arathi. Leaders

---

[22]This was the judgment of Kenyatta in *Facing Mount Kenya*, 271.

[23]Githieya, *Freedom of the Spirit*, 45, 47, 51. "It was believed that through their employment, these
families would be brought under constant Christian contact" (p. 47).

[24]Ibid., 123-24. Immediately after this experience Joseph secluded himself for three years of Bible
reading, prayer, and fasting. See pp. 125-27.

[25]Kimathi Samuel notes that the colonial administration refused to recognize traditional authority.
"Akorino Church," 3.

[26]This point is emphasized by Githieya, *Freedom of the Spirit*, 123.

would often retreat to isolated areas to study and reflect on these Scriptures, following the example of both Paul and their first bishop, Joseph; soon groups of traveling evangelists arose to preach and nurture congregations. Each congregational center featured two *gaaru* (barracks), one for men and another for women, where they gathered for worship and various other activities. Their distinctive worship featured traditional music, drumming, and loud emotional prayers. Arathi elders typically carried a white bag slung over their shoulders containing religious literature and instructions on doctrine and practice.

The structure of these groups, while informed by biblical teaching, reflected the traditional African family or homestead. The father functioned as the family priest, and all the family participated together in worship, both in homes and in corporate worship in the *gaaru*. Their worship, however, reflects not only the traditional social structure but also, inevitably, its religious inheritance. In traditional religious practice, the Gikuyu worshiped Ngai, the creator of all things who was thought to dwell in the sky but comes to earth and visits Mount Kenya and so is addressed as *Mwene-Nyaga* (owner of the mountain of brightness, Mount Kenya). Thus the Akorino face this sacred mountain when they pray. Sacrifices to Mwene-Nyaga were made by the council of elders, who stood apart from the rest of the people by their purity and power. They were thought to have special powers. Kenyatta wrote of these elders:

> The *Watu wa Mungu* (people of God) . . . assume the role of holy men, they claim to be in direct communication with *Mwene-Nyaga* (God). They claim, too, that *Mwene-Nyaga* has given them power to know the past and present, and to interpret his message to the community at large, hence their name Arathi. . . . Their prayers are a mixture of Gikuyu and Christian; in these they add something new to both religions.[27]

The divine powers given by the Holy Spirit are never to be used for personal purposes, but only for the welfare of the community. For it is feared that if anyone dared to misuse such powers, thus acting contrary to Mwene-Nyaga's instructions, the result would be disaster, not only to himself but to the whole of his family. These elders often took over the role of traditional healers as well, receiving from God instructions about what herbs to use for which ailment.

---

[27]Kenyatta, *Facing Mount Kenya*, 273-74.

Prophets in Africa have long played a central role in bringing spiritual messages. One such prophet was Mūgo wa Kībirū, who in the late nineteenth century prophesied about the coming of the Europeans. According to the traditional account, Mūgo wa Kībirū had pled with God to spare his people this unwanted invasion, to the extent of wrestling unsuccessfully with God. Afterward, bruised and exhausted, Mūgo wa Kībirū finally obeyed Ngai's command to warn the people. He described their clothes and their strength and warned that opposition would be fatal for them. And their coming would be the beginning of suffering, not only for them but also for neighboring tribes. As predicted, about the time the Europeans began to arrive in great numbers, between 1889 and 1892, a rinderpest epidemic swept through East Africa killing up to 90 percent of their cattle, a catastrophe that was followed by a severe famine, which the people came to call the Famine of Europe.[28]

After their reading of the New Testament, the Arathi assumed that the special power they previously attributed to Mūgo wa Kībirū was really sourced in the biblical God and that the Holy Spirit was the true source of the wisdom they saw in the elders and their practices. They also assumed that the miracles performed by Jesus and the apostles would be continued in their own communities through the mediation of the elders, an expectation that in many cases was fulfilled. They were particularly attracted to the eschatological vision of the New Testament and so originally owned no property (though this has changed over time—just as it did in the early church), and they refrained from any involvement in politics in order to devote themselves entirely to their religious life.

Akorinos shake and call out in tongues when praying, believing they are in direct contact with the Holy Spirit—whom they received at baptism. The teaching of Scripture informs the whole of their life, from marriage through specific burial practices—though their often literal reading of Scripture is filtered through the lens of their inherited culture and religious practices. Jacob Kimathi Samuel notes that the Akorino Church represents a critical example of a fresh encounter of traditional culture with the teaching of Scripture, by people who were obedient to what they believed to be God's word in Scripture

---

[28]This history is recounted in Solomon Wachira Waigwa, "Pentecost Without Azusa: An Historical and Theological Account of the Akorino Church in Kenya" (PhD diss., 1991), cited by Kimathi Samuel, "Akorino Church," 6.

and in their own personal experience. To their minds, the missionaries were not taking Scripture seriously enough because they did not obey the Old Testament—which for the Akorinos resonated so deeply with their own culture. Meanwhile they saw missionaries as simply mediators of Western culture. Sadly, missionaries, for their part, dismissed movements like the Akorinos as sub-Christian, and the opportunity for mutual learning was lost. As Kenyatta describes this, "Very offensive and unedifying attacks were made, in the name of Christ, on the Christian neighbors of missionaries. But nothing was done to investigate the religious aspects of this group, to show the connection between it and Christianity on the one hand and Gikuyu religion on the other."[29]

Citing the late Ghanaian theologian Kwame Bediako, Jacob Kimathi observes, with a touch of irony, that Christianity is often thought to be shallow in Africa—a mile wide and an inch deep. Could this be, he wonders, because Christianity did not confront the African worldview and appropriate the resources of its traditional faith? As Bediako notes, Christianity often failed to meet the Akan (his own Ghanaian ethnicity) in the terms of its inherited spirituality. Consequently, the Christian communities that have resulted can only relate to their past by distancing themselves from it.[30] Surely this has something to do with the nominal character of much of African Christianity. Bediako insists that only to the extent that a believing community appropriates its own spiritual heritage will it have the resources to show the relevance of Christ for that place. It must depend on developing its own oral and vernacular expressions of faith, nourished by the resources of indigenous spirituality, as well as the teaching of Scripture and the power of the Spirit.[31]

Unlike the West, which has divided life into segments and relegated the spiritual life to an increasingly smaller compartment, Africans pray "without ceasing," whether dedicating a new house, pleading for healing, or seeking success in exams—giving evidence, Bediako notes, of an essentially unified and "spiritual" universe. Education and modernization in Africa have not succeeded in displacing this fundamental conviction that, as Jacob Kimathi puts

---

[29]Kenyatta, *Facing Mount Kenya*, 279. In part because of this continuing opposition, their subsequent history was troubled. Though several attempts at consolidation were made, Githieya observes, "no unity of doctrine or practice was ever achieved." Githieya, *Freedom of the Spirit*, 138.

[30]Kwame Bediako, *Christianity in Africa: A Renewal of a Non-Christian Religion* (Maryknoll, NY: Orbis Books, 1995).

[31]Ibid., 86.

it, "God is an inner necessity for humankind."[32] Though the Akorinos were quick to recognize the radical revelation of God, of Ngai, in Jesus Christ, they were nevertheless convinced that this "news" was only describing further what the African people already knew about God. They also were persuaded that whatever else it meant, it did not imply that they needed to give up their identity as Africans, and their religious experience was a potential site for expanding the lexicon of Christian theology. As an example, consider how the Akorino leaders immediately interpreted their original visions as a baptism of the Holy Spirit—just as in the book of Acts believers' experience with God came first; theological reflection followed.

But notice as well how Akorinos understood and practiced their faith. They saw this not as translating some message into their setting but as obedience to the Scriptures they read and to the visions that constituted, for them, a direct call from God. These visions and the inspirited world they represent were not merely prejudices to be overcome; they provided the idiom and the impetus in terms of which this gospel would be construed and lived out in that place—if, that is, it was not to remain a foreign import.

In one sense neither of these case studies directly represents insider movements, but they contain critical lessons for our approach to these. First, it is important to recognize that religious traditions are not homogenous but are fractured arenas of spiritual conflict. Surely violence and corruption must be opposed and overthrown; at the same time, within the impulses for peace and reconciliation—the angels of our better nature—God's presence and work may be discerned. But second, God is still in the business of speaking to people, and, when this is accompanied by conversation with Scripture, new forms of faith and discipleship can be forged. They are found, that is, if we are willing and able, like Peter in Acts 10, to free ourselves from our inherited religious assumptions. These lessons I want to draw out further in what follows.

EMERGENT MOVEMENTS IN ASIA:
INDIA, SOUTHEAST ASIA, AND THE PHILIPPINES

We turn our attention now to Asia, which represents a unique situation of cultural and religious diversity that, from the beginning, has issued in a wide

---

[32]Kimathi Samuel, "Akorino Church," 14.

variety of responses to the Christian message. Asia is also the region where, for the most part, Christianity is not only a minority religion but is frequently identified as a foreign import. And here too is where one encounters the most serious divide between typical Western appeals to recruit more missionaries and mobilize additional resources to evangelize Asia (cf. programs associated with the so-called 10-40 Window, addressing the area between 10 and 40 degrees north of the equator), and the increasing number of indigenous voices (both Catholic and evangelical) calling for new forms of mission in Asia. These voices seek to define mission in terms of Christian presence, "not as outsiders who drop by sporadically to visit and then leave, but as insiders who remain bound in solidarity and empathy with [their neighbors]."[33] It is not surprising then that Asia provides significant examples of emergent forms of Christian presence that have sparked the most discussion and controversy.

The major characteristic of the missional situation of Asia is the Christian encounter with the great religious traditions and the cultures formed by those traditions—a circumstance that is arguably more pressing, and more inescapable, in Asia than in any other region. As Asian Christians remind outsiders, Asians (with the possible exception of Christians in parts of the Philippines) grow up in a religiously diverse world in which interaction with adherents of other faith traditions is a normal part of life—they are friends, neighbors, and family members. Difference is natural to them. Therefore, while practicing their faith, they are faced at many points with interreligious challenges requiring delicate negotiations. I have long been struck by the way Asian reflection on mission frames the discussion in ways that seem strange—even dangerous—to outsiders. The pronouncements of the Federation of Asian Bishops' Conferences (FABC) of the Catholic Church offer a good example of such reflection. Over the past generation the FABC has given sustained attention to its missionary situation. In their statements they have sought to express the difficulties (and the joys) of their context—often in ways that Rome itself has found perplexing. This excerpt from its "Theses on Interreligious Dialogue" (1987) is worth quoting at length:

---

[33]Jonathan Tan, *Christian Mission Among the Peoples of Asia* (Maryknoll, NY: Orbis Books, 2014), 106. Tan's study is an excellent introduction not only to the missional situation in Asia but to the Catholic response in particular.

In the course of the last two thousand years the Church has encountered and dialogued with various peoples, cultures and religions, with varying levels of success. Today, however, especially in Asia, in the context of the Great Religions, which are in the process of revival and renewal, the Church is aware of a markedly different situation. We do not ask any longer about the relationship of the Church to other cultures and religions. We are rather searching for the place and role of the Church in a religiously and culturally pluralistic world.[34]

Notice the change from reflection on the "relationship" of the church to other religions, which allows for abstract inquiries, to trying to discern the "place and role" of the church, something that calls for concrete responses and practices. This unique situation forces deliberation and modes of engagement that seek ways of living in and with difference, of seeing this as an opportunity for learning and growth and not as a problem to be overcome. It is not surprising then that many of the most important "insider" movements have occurred in Asia, and it is for this reason we focus most of our attention there.

As implied in the theses quoted above, in the mind of many Christian leaders the traditional forms of mission have not worked very well. Kang-San Tan, director of Asia Church Mission Society (AsiaCMS), has argued that "for over two hundred years the Evangelical approach of trying to replace other religions with Christianity has not been successful."[35] We need to recover, he thinks, a deep sense of sharing a common humanity and, most importantly, to seek to understand other religious traditions on their own terms while discovering a new role for our Christian witness. What can we learn about this new role from case studies in Asia?

a. India. In India in particular there is a long history dating back to the nineteenth century of followers of Christ who, for various reasons, resisted joining Christian churches.[36] In spite of three hundred years of Christian presence, a dominant characteristic of the Christian church in India remains

---

[34]Theological Advisory Commission of the Federation of Asian Bishops (FABC), "Theses on Interreligious Dialogue: An Essay in Pastoral Theological Reflection," approved April 1987, introduction, para. 0.8, quoted in Jonathan Tan, *Christian Mission Among the Peoples of Asia*, 101.

[35]Kang-San Tan, "Beyond Demonising Religions: A Biblical Framework for Interfaith Relations in Asia," *Church and Society in Asia Today* 15 (December 2012): 188; cf. 191.

[36]Scholars of the period note that these early efforts can hardly be called movements since they seldom outlived their founders, though they constitute important precedents. See the discussion in Darren Todd Duerksen, *Ecclesial Identities in a Multi-Faith Context: Jesus Truth-Gatherings (Yeshu Satsangs) Among Hindus and Sikhs in Northwest India* (Eugene, OR: Pickwick, 2015), 3-30.

its foreignness.[37] Early in the twentieth century Sadhu Sundar Singh noticed many Hindus who had become followers of Christ but who refused to identify themselves as Christian. He noted that some kept their faith secret for strategic reasons, but most did so out of the low estimation they had of Christians and the church and the desire not to be alienated from their families and communities. Of these Singh says: "I do not agree that they are right in not coming out openly, yet I have never been able to feel that they are not Christians."[38] Singh pointed out that believers in Christ faced difficulties whether they separated from their communities or not, but concluded that "it would have been better if, instead of separating new converts from their friends and relatives, they had been allowed to stay on in their old homes. Then they would have been stronger through the struggle and persecution they would have had to face."[39] This is a remarkable comment, for it implies that remaining in your traditional setting is not a way to escape religious persecution, as is often believed, but a way to prepare for this—which Singh supposes will be the necessary result of following Christ in any case.

More recently, the well-known Indian theologian M. M. Thomas (1916–1996), after an evangelical conversion, came to believe that the redemption that Christ brought about must be understood in the broader perspective of the Indian struggle for human rights and justice. In 1971 in his book *Salvation and Humanisation*, he published a remarkable testimony of the failure of Christian missions in India and the ways it needed to change. The fundamental problem, he noted, is that Christianity has seen itself as a separate community alongside other religious communities in India. What is worse, it has presented itself as a closed community, shut off in mission compounds, that seeks to control the whole of believers' lives. As a result baptism is widely perceived as repudiating one's ancient heritage and accepting an alien culture.[40]

---

[37]This generalization applies to the churches resulting during this period from the modern missionary movement. Christianity had an earlier, and more indigenous, presence in what is known as the Mar Thoma Church in the Southwest of India, which dates back to the early centuries of the Christian era.

[38]Sadhu Sundar Singh, *With and Without Christ* (New York: Harper, 1929), 29. On the various motivations for secrecy, see pp. 32-44.

[39]Ibid., 52.

[40]M. M. Thomas, *Salvation and Humanisation: Some Crucial Issues of the Theology of Mission in Contemporary India* (Madras: Christian Institute on the Study of Religion and Society, 1971), 14, 60.

He wondered: Can we move beyond the understanding of Christianity as another (mostly foreign) religious community?[41] Can we see Christ as the bearer of a "new community in India"? For this to happen, Thomas argued, the church must take new forms, in which a Christian self-identity is combined with a secular solidarity with all people. Why cannot the legitimate goal of Indian missions be a "Christ-centered Hindu Church of Christ which transforms Hindu and life patterns from within?"[42] In many ways Thomas anticipated the many insider movements that have flourished since that time.

Similarly, Aloysius Pieris, a Jesuit scholar, has argued over the last three decades that the whole approach of inculturation makes little sense in Asian society. This is because it too often means the insertion of "the Christian religion minus European culture" into an "Asian culture minus non-Christian religion."[43] This, he thinks, is inconceivable in the South Asian context. In contrast, he proposes what he calls "inreligionization," in which believers in Christ allow themselves to be "baptized in the Jordan River of Asian religions."[44] By this he means that the liberation that Christ brings must be expressed in the Asian idiom that has been forged over the centuries in the great religious traditions. He summarizes this process: Asians "will not spontaneously embark on a costly adventure unless their lives are touched and their depths stirred by its prospects *along the 'cultural' patterns of their own 'religious histories.'*"[45]

Such ideas, though widespread (and mostly opposed by missionaries and traditional churches), did not come to the attention of the larger missiological communities until the 1970s when, after the publication of Thomas's book, Lesslie Newbigin and Thomas began a correspondence that came to be known as the Thomas-Newbigin debates.[46] Thomas argued that though the traditional churches are the visible face of God's kingdom, there is no reason that fellowships of Christ followers cannot exist outside of such visible forms and still be a part of the kingdom of God. Newbigin, while acknowledging the difficult nature of the social situation of the church in India, felt the New Testament

---

[41]Ibid., 39-40; see also p. 16.

[42]Ibid., 60; see also p. 40.

[43]Aloysius Pieris, *An Asian Theology of Liberation* (Maryknoll, NY: Orbis Books, 1988), 52. He notes that "these Indian theologians and their colleagues in the West are working with different paradigms."

[44]Ibid., 113.

[45]Ibid., 100, emphasis original.

[46]See Duerksen, *Ecclesial Identities*, 12-13, and the literature cited there.

had no room for those who "mentally and spiritually" followed Christ but did not belong to the human relationships embodied in church fellowships.

During this period the debate was responding largely to anecdotal and personal encounters, such as those described by Sundar Singh or Thomas. But somewhat later Herbert E. Hoefer began to study the phenomenon based on qualitative and quantitative methods and in 2001 published his influential book on *Churchless Christianity*.[47] Hoefer studied the presence of groups who followed Christ without identifying with the Christian church and concluded that there were legitimate ecclesial expressions that did not visibly identify with the Christian church. He called such believers nonbaptized believers in Christ. Subsequently, students of Asian mission have begun to follow up on Hoefer's research.

My focus here will be on a recent study of what are called *Yeshu Satsangs* (lit. "Jesus devotees") in the Punjab (northwest India), research conducted by Darren Duerksen between 2006 and 2009.[48] Duerksen's study is based on interviews with several communities of Hindus and Sikhs who have become followers of Christ. The study is placed firmly in the context of the pluralism that exists in India today in two respects. On the one hand, it takes its start from the obvious fact that there are a wide variety of "Christian" ecclesial identities in India today, representing both the diversity of (mostly Western) Christian denominations and the many ecclesial movements that have been intentionally formed over against the traditional Christian churches. Since the nineteenth century, Duerksen notes, despite the vaunted two-thousand-year history of Christianity in India and the fact that churches are now led by Indians, "Christianity's foreign reputation and the competitive contradiction that this represents continues to persist."[49] As a result, new forms of Christ followers have begun to appear. Hoefer and others have called attention to aspects of these emerging communities, but no one has studied in depth their

---

[47]Herbert E. Hoefer, *Churchless Christianity* (Pasadena, CA: William Carey Library, 2001). The research was carried out in the 1970s and 1980s and surveyed more than eight hundred people. See Duerksen, *Ecclesial Identities*, 10-11.

[48]Duerksen studied six *Yeshu Satsangs* (four in Hindu villages, and two in Sikh villages) by interviewing six leaders and fifty members of these communities as well as carrying out participant observation in their services of worship. In this part of India, Hindu and Sikh communities are closely related, sharing strong cultural and historical connections. Duerksen describes his method in *Ecclesial Identities*, chap. 3.

[49]Ibid., 64.

communal self-identity—that is, no one has asked whether, as believers in Christ, they consider themselves "church," and if they do, how they understand this.[50] This Duerksen sets out to examine.

On the other hand, Duerksen's study recognizes the parallel diversity in expressions and understandings of what it means to be Hindu. Hinduism has historically been understood as an amalgam of a wide variety of beliefs and practices without any central control or consistent social contour. As a result, Hindu identity, somewhat like the contrasting "Christian identity," has been fluid—causing observers to ask whether it is merely a cultural phenomenon or a "social construct."[51] At the same time, some practitioners of Hinduism who have become followers of Christ have recognized the possibility of separating the social dharma from the personal and devotional dharma, allowing one to follow the first without the second.[52] The question then arises, to what extent are such groups still Hindu? Such questions, arising often from within Hinduism itself, give some indication of the difficulty of describing, let alone evaluating, contemporary movements.

The special contribution of Duerksen's study is to make the unstable and developing nature of these groups a special object of reflection. He does this by paying close attention to what he calls their "ecclesial identities," that is, how and to what degree they have begun to see themselves as members of a special community based on their faith in Christ. Ecclesial identities, he proposes, "consist of shared practices formed over the course of time through interactions between members' contexts and their faith in Christ."[53] Notice the focus on practices and relationships, which he argues provide a more fruitful opening than a focus on structure. In order to take advantage of the developmental character of these groups, he appropriates an emergent theory of agency,

---

[50]It may have been symptomatic of Western research methods that previous studies have focused on nonbaptized believers rather than on communities of faith. This is a special strength of Duerksen's study.

[51]Part of the argument of the next chapter will be to show that terms like *Hinduism* and *Christianity* are mostly useless in communicating any fixed content. In a helpful article, H. L. Richard calls these terms empty concepts that must simply be discarded. See Richard, "Religious Syncretism as a Syncretistic Concept: The Inadequacy of the 'World Religions' Paradigm," in *Understanding Insider Movements: Disciples of Jesus in Diverse Communities*, ed. Harley Talman and John Jay Travis (Pasadena, CA: William Carey Library, 2015), 363-74, esp. 371.

[52]*Dharma* is a Sanskrit word meaning "law" or "behavior that is considered to be in accord with the order of things." See the study in Duerksen, *Ecclesial Identities*, 6.

[53]Ibid., 31.

which draws on the work of Pierre Bourdieu and Margaret Archer. According to this theory, decisions and projects are a mix of reflection on ideas about God's presence and work, together with inherited dispositions that people bring with them. People cultivate habits that consciously or unconsciously draw from the cultural repertoire at hand, as well as the specific teachings of a new faith. This collection of dispositions, cultural resources, and theological awareness, Duerksen argues, displays emergent properties providing both constraint and enablement for people to develop new roles and identities.[54]

These groups must be seen, then, not as fixed but as entities that are gradually emerging. Practices and relationships forming over time give these groups a unique and evolving character. Interestingly, all the leaders of these groups came to faith and were discipled in traditional Christian churches. But all of them over time grew dissatisfied with the worship of these churches and formed groups that transitioned into the Yeshu Satsang style.

What is the Yeshu Satsang style? The starting point, not surprisingly, comes from the Hindu and Sikh practices common to the Punjab religious landscape. The style appropriates the familiar *bhajans* style of music widely popular in Hindu and Sikh bhakti traditions.[55] Respondents stressed that this music was an important means of evoking family and social memories as well as serving as a suitable vehicle of praise to God. Then there is the peaceful setting of the Sikh temple (*gurdwara*), which they seek to replicate in their gatherings. Listen to Jasbir's reference to Sikh prayer: "Our Sikh style, I like their way of praying. We [the Christian church] are too loud. . . . They are well behaved people in their *satsangs*. . . . I think if we will bring that level of spirituality which they profess . . . in *gurdwaras* to the churches, the churches can be transformed."[56] There are also various significant objects, such as the incense- or coconut-burning *diya* (oil lamp) familiar to Hindu communities (though not to the Sikh community). And there are behaviors deemed appropriate to these cultures, such as the removal of shoes when inside, women wearing veils, or Sikhs retaining their beards and turbans. All of these can be used, they argue, to show that followers of Jesus have not ceased being Indian or left their Indian

---

[54]Ibid., 28, 37-41.

[55]Ibid., 74-75. The *bhakti* tradition of Hinduism, dating to the medieval period, stresses a personal and inward devotion to God as a way of becoming one with God (thus representing a stream of Hinduism that believes in a personal God).

[56]Ibid., 77. Cf. also p. 79 for a description of religious objects.

heritage behind. They seek in other words to retain a level of solidarity with their Hindu and Sikh communities—even if direct self-ascription as Hindu in some cases is problematic. They are still part of the Hindu community, still Sikh (which literally means "learning"). Outside of worship they are comfortable attending functions in the (Sikh and Hindu) temples and making Hindu offerings (*prasad*)—though they emphatically forbid idol worship. As Duerksen describes this process, he notes the Satsangi leaders must constrain the religio-structural associations even as they redefine them.[57]

But these practices are all inscribed, Duerksen argues, with new emergent properties, new beliefs about Christ that, in their minds, complete the message of their Hindu or Sikh scriptures. And this encourages specific practices associated with these properties. Duerksen notes four such practices evident in his study: use of the Bible, the Lord's Supper, baptism, and certain speech practices. Though these practices are shared with the traditional Christian churches, the Satsangis seek to disassociate their practices from the structure of those churches. The Bible, or *Yeshu bani* (Jesus' word), is central to their worship. As Ravi, one of the leaders, notes, attendance at the temple or using the *bhajans* will not get you to heaven. "God's word is the thing that changes peoples' hearts, but [the *satsang* practice] helps us to keep relationships with people."[58]

Frequently these believers maintain their respect for Hindu (or Sikh) writings, though for them the Scriptures are the ultimate and higher authority. As Dinesh put this: "The Bible is the conclusion of all."[59] They read it openly in their meetings, and it is the focus of their sermons. The Lord's Supper (*Prabhu Bhoj*) is commonly practiced in the Yeshu Satsangs and is freely offered to all; they typically stress its connection with the sufferings of the Lord. Guarav, one of the leaders, says: "Jesus wants us to have communion, to share the suffering that he went through. So this *Prabhu Bhoj* reminds us that we have to face suffering when we follow Christ."[60] Baptism, because it is typically associated in India with the radical change of religious community, is deemphasized in the *satsangs*. For them, baptism is not the pivotal experience it is for other Indian Christians; rather, some miracle or healing often provides

---

[57]Ibid., 89, 90, 115, 125.
[58]Ibid., 117-18. On their separation from Christian structures, see p. 127.
[59]Ibid., 130.
[60]Ibid., 131.

the spark that prompts them to follow Christ and become part of the *satsang*. These become pivotal experiences. In speech practices *satsangis* seek to find self-ascriptions that do not have associations with the Christian churches, such as calling themselves *Yeshu Bhaktas*, a designation that underlines their solidarity with Hindu culture.[61]

But what sets these groups apart as communities that follow Jesus? In what ways do they conceive of these "projects" as ecclesial spaces? In his analysis of the data collected from these six communities, Duerksen discovered four prominent and interrelated themes.[62] First, they all experienced a bhakti-influenced devotion to Jesus. The prayers and *bhajans* allow them to experience a deep and personal connection to Jesus, as expressed in this well-known *bhajan*:

> Keep the lamp burning so the Lord's name will remain.
> Remain in my (inner) temple, remain in my temple.
> In the morning and in the evening my soul sings your name, Jesus.
> Lord Jesus, your name,
> Let your name remain in my soul.[63]

Second, this devotion is often connected with the experience of God's blessing and power. Prayers and sermons often return to the theme of the power of the Holy Spirit to heal, to deliver them from evil, and to forgive their sins. Third, this is related to an awareness and careful discernment of evil—even deliverance from evil spirits and powers. Finally, this leads to an identity marker that leaders mentioned most frequently, that is, the desire to be a witness to their Hindu and Sikh communities.[64]

These characteristics provide markers that describe an emergent process that is not fully a part of the Christian communities around it nor fully Hindu or Sikh. This careful description marks a significant advance over previous churchless research. In an important chapter, Duerksen makes use of this same emergent theory to analyze the emerging church in the book of Acts. He concludes that at the end of Acts these communities were *both* a Jewish sect and a distinct community called "the Way."[65] And the leaders themselves did

---

[61]Ibid., 137.
[62]Ibid., 146.
[63]Ibid., 147.
[64]Ibid., 148-51.
[65]Ibid., 247.

not know whether these groups represented transitional spaces or something more permanent. In a sense this did not matter, for they represented communities who clearly followed Christ and who demonstrated in their individual and corporate lives the renewing work of God centered in Christ and empowered by the Holy Spirit.

I especially want to emphasize that shifting attention away from the ways in which the gospel can be contextualized in these communities, and attending to the emergent interaction between the qualities of the gospel and the communities inherited dispositions, allows a new, generative space to come into view—what Sundermeier has called *convivencia*. In this new hermeneutical space a new form of Christian discipleship becomes possible, and along the way new insight into both the work of Christ and the value of Hindu and Sikh practices emerges. Though it is not possible to know how these groups will develop in the future, it is not hard to imagine that communities like this may represent a better future for the gospel in India.

b. Buddhist communities in Southeast Asia. In the country of Thailand the Christian church does not have the long history that it has in India. But over the last two centuries a vigorous Thai church has emerged as a minority movement within an overwhelmingly Theravada Buddhist culture. However, though these groups share the same (Thai) language, they often appear to live in different worlds. As a husband-and-wife pastoral team has noted recently, over the nearly two-hundred-year history of the Thai church, Christian terms have developed that are incomprehensible to Buddhists in Thailand.[66] They conclude: "Christians expect Buddhists to comprehend our Christian message the same way as we do, without realizing that a Buddhist's interpretation will be according to the Buddhist worldview. Thus our good news is not good news to Buddhists."[67] For example, *bap* has come to be the accepted Thai word for "sin," but for Buddhists there is no such notion as sin. Rather, *bap* means "black," or "unskilled actions" (*kamma*) that hinder one from reaching *nibbana* (Nirvana).[68]

As a result, many Southeast Asian Buddhists are exploring the possibility of dual religious belonging that combines a primary allegiance to Christ with

---

[66]Bantoon Boon-Itt and Mai Boon-Itt, "Bridging Buddhist Christian Worldview: Communicating in Context for Theravada Buddhist Breakthrough," *Mission Frontiers* 36, no. 6 (2014): 15-19.
[67]Ibid., 16.
[68]Ibid., 17.

a secondary affiliation to one's traditional religion. AsiaCMS mission director and theologian Kang-San Tan describes this as a "framework which enables . . . Christians to incorporate some aspect of their non-Christian faiths, as long as they do not contradict the basic tenets of Christian orthodoxy."[69] This would allow converts from Buddhism to participate in Buddhist marriage and funeral ceremonies and to pay visits to the temple with family members.

Evidence of insider movements in this part of Asia remains scarce, but one that has gained attention, in the Isaan region of Eastern Thailand, apparently represents thousands of Buddhists who have come to Christ. These converts call themselves the New Buddhists. Banpote Wetchgama, a leader instrumental in this movement, has argued that Buddhists feel they must follow the way of their ancestors just as New Testament Jews chose to retain their Jewish heritage.[70] To ask these Buddhists to leave their tradition is not only an insult to their families and society but actually undermines their identity. Moreover, since Christianity is invariably perceived as a foreign religion, it cannot simply be added to the amalgam of beliefs that make up popular Buddhism. But why not allow people to come to Christ without asking them to leave behind these traditions, even if they will understand these differently in the fresh light of Scripture?

These believers call themselves New Buddhists, not *Khris-tee-yen*, the Thai word for Christian. Why New Buddhists? Because, Wetchgama argues, Buddhism as it exists is incomplete; its followers have not received full salvation. And, because their progress depends on their own efforts, they have come to realize they cannot keep the teachings of Buddha.[71] But here is the good news for them: Jesus has brought *nibbana* to them! Jesus offers release from the suffering that human desires have caused. The root of sin is to cling to what is mine—as a Thai proverb has it: "What is mine is mine, the source of suffering." But none of us can escape from this cycle; God has come in Jesus to deliver us from death by his suffering and resurrection. Notice that for these believers the teaching of Buddha is still to be respected, but it will now be seen in the

[69]Kang-San Tan, "An Examination of Dual Religious Belonging Theology: Contributions to Evangelical Missiology" (PhD diss., University of Aberdeen, 2014), 203. Tan, born into a Buddhist family, has sought to reconnect with them through shared practices.
[70]The leader Banpote Wetchgama wrote an extensive report in Thai, portions of which were translated and published as "The New Buddhists: How Buddhists Can Follow Christ," *Mission Frontiers* 36, no. 6 (2014): 28-31.
[71]Ibid., 30-31.

light of Scripture, which opens a new way to achieve *nibbana*. They are called New Buddhists, Wetchgama insists, because they have allowed the teachings of Christ to be reborn in a Buddhist context; they "can easily explain release from sin and suffering using the teachings of Buddha himself."

As with Yeshu Satsangs, a primary characteristic of this movement is the desire to witness to Christ in that place. Wetchgama notes that he never tells people he is a Christian, for that would immediately close the door to further conversation. Why would he do that? He tells them that he is a New Buddhist, which invariably prompts the question of how New Buddhism is different from the old Buddhism. This gives him the opportunity to testify that, before, he depended on his own efforts, but now he depends on the grace of God expressed in Jesus Christ. This enables him not only to testify to Christ's liberation but also to use Buddhist teachings on Enlightenment to challenge the idolatrous animist practices, which Buddha also rejected, and to describe the joy-filled life that Christ offers and the prospect of being with God after death. He concludes:

> For Eastern people, to understand and accept the heart of the Gospel without any barriers, we must allow the good news, or the *thamma*, to be reborn in the forms and cultural expressions of Eastern people.[72]

For these believers, the teachings of Buddha find a new setting, and new resonance, when they are understood in the light of the gospel. They provide terms in which the gospel can be seen and accepted. But notice that these terms are not a ladder that is climbed and then discarded but a permanent starting point and a continuing orientation for rethinking the renewing work of God in Christ. Notice too the inclination to return to the book of Acts for guidance in these emerging situations. As with the Yeshu Satsangs, distinctive elements emerge that characterize movements in widely different settings: a consistent focus on devotion to Christ, an impulse to share this good news with family and friends, and regular recourse to learning from Scripture. Paul DeNeui offers an additional characteristic of these movements that is relevant to our overall claim. Insider Buddhist communities, he notes, "are comprised entirely of believers who come from folk Buddhism, know little about Western

---

[72]Wetchgama, "New Buddhists," 31. *Thamma* is the truth taught by Buddha, which comes very close, he thinks, to the Greek notion of the Logos.

forms of Christianity, and are not learning about them or adopting them."[73] In other words, these groups represent not an incursion from outside but an impulse of the Spirit from within.

c. The Magindanon believers of the southern Philippines. Our final case study comes from the southern island of Mindanao in the Philippines, which for centuries has been the home of indigenous people groups that are traditionally Muslim. Over the past several generations there has arisen a movement of people whose respective identities are defined not by their Filipino nationality but by their identity as people groups who continue to observe Islam while expressing allegiance to a faith in *Isa al Masih* (Jesus Christ).[74]

The particular historical and political setting is crucial for understanding both these people and the movement of those who follow Christ. Centuries ago this lower part of Southeast Asia, the swath of islands stretching down from Malaysia through Indonesia and into the southern islands of what is now the Philippines, converted to Islam (representing to this day the area with the largest concentration of Muslims in the world). In the twentieth century a series of Filipino presidents, in an attempt to subjugate the violent population of what were called Moros, began a series of "land reforms," which essentially involved giving over large parcels of land to immigrants from other parts of the Philippines. This entailed introducing political and economic practices that ignored centuries-long indigenous traditions and sparked deep-seated (and often violent) opposition by the people to the central government in Manila. After years of struggle, and on-and-off negotiation, in October 2012 a Framework Agreement of the Bangsamoro (the name for this newly autonomous region) was signed, signaling the beginning of a three-year period of preparation for the implementation of the Basic Laws, providing a form of self-governance and allowing for a nonsubjugated Muslimhood.[75]

Significant for our purposes is the continuing antipathy these Muslim groups feel both toward the Manila government and toward Christianity,

---

[73]Paul DeNeui, "A Typology of Approaches to Folk Buddhists," in Charles H. Kraft, *Appropriate Christianity* (Pasadena, CA: William Carey Library, 2005), 428.

[74]The Arabic phrase *Isa al Masih* means "Jesus the Messiah," or "Jesus the Christ." The principal source for this section is the article by E. Acoba (pseudonym), "Towards an Understanding of Inclusivity in Contextualizing into Philippine Context," in *The Gospel in Culture: Contextualization Issues Through Asian Eyes*, ed. Melba Padilla Maggay (Manila: OMF Literature/ISACC, 2013), 416-50.

[75]Ibid., 422.

identified as it is with this painful history of subjugation. In this context, during the last century four Muslim leaders who became followers of Christ began to form their own *da'wah* (a community of people who follow the teachings of Jesus), and these eventually met and formed a loose federation they call IMC (Indigenous Movement Communities).[76] There is now a third generation of believers from these groups who come together regularly to fellowship and reflect on their lives as Muslims who follow Christ. They intentionally guard against religious practices identified as Christian, whether this is construction of church buildings or following a religious liturgy that reflects the Christian tradition. During a recent colloquium, the leaders asked the group, composed mostly of younger believers, to formulate a working definition of the *da'wah*. After some discussion the participants defined *da'wah* as "inviting others to the way of righteousness." Many of the older leaders were amazed at this constructive formulation because it revealed that the younger generation had not inherited the negative baggage of the older leaders toward expatriate missionary strategies and practices. While they still insisted on maintaining their independence from the "churches," many of them were able to express appreciation for what the missionaries had done and, more importantly, they were able to begin the positive process of constructing their own local missionary theology. The natural process of their theological development is instructive. During their consultations, participants were asked to suggest topics they considered important for further discussion, and a majority voiced the desire to study the prophets, given the centrality of prophecy to Muslim faith. So they scheduled a workshop dedicated to this discussion, and seventy-five participants attended. Khalid, the facilitator, had passages read from the Qur'an dealing with prophecy.[77] A passage from the Qur'an declares: "It is He Who sent down to thee (step by step) in truth the Book confirming what went before it: and He sent down Law (of Moses) and the Gospel (of Jesus) before this as a guide to mankind" (Q ʿImrōn 3:3). Khalid further pointed to Q Baqarah 2:87: "We gave Moses the Book and followed him up with a succession of Apostles: We gave Jesus the son of Mary clear (signs) and strengthened him with the holy spirit." Another read from Q Baqarah 2:136: "We believe in Allah and the revelation given to us and to

---

[76]Ibid., 423-24.
[77]Ibid., 427-28.

Abraham . . . and that given to Moses and Jesus." They all saw the importance of studying these prophets, both in the Qur'an and in the *Kitab* (Bible) and *Injil* (Gospels), to receive guidance for a "way that is straight" (a reference to Q Baqarah 2:140-42).

At a critical point Khalid recalled the story of the *al-Miraj* (the ascension of the Prophet Muhammad narrated in the Hadith, the collected oral traditions of Muhammad's teachings—though the event is also referred to in the Qur'an). Khalid was insistent that their study of prophecy be carried out within the framework of this essential narrative—authorizing Muhammad's prophetic role in the teaching that originated with Muhammad, which Khalid argued provided equal space to learn about all the prophets. Through this process of exploring the nature of prophecy in the light of Muhammad's teaching, the facilitators were able to show clearly that Jesus, *Isa al Masih*, was central in the tradition of the prophets. In this way they were making their way toward a Christology that emerged out of the Islamic narrative itself, rather than one imposed by a master narrative of Christian theology. Acoba acknowledges that evangelicals are likely to view this process as syncretism, but he thinks such a judgment fails to recognize the unique hermeneutical process shaped by these Muslim Magindanon believers. Acoba claims this process "also presses towards an acceptance that the gospel narrative is not the domain of the evangelical enterprise alone. In other words, the local practice of hermeneutics is constructing its own narrative of the gospel based on local religious narratives."[78]

This unique interpretive move, I believe, does more than merely suggest the construction of a local theology, though it does this as well. Outside observers should guard against projecting their own religious prejudices on narratives of this kind—whether in judgment or approbation. The truth is that theological formulations simply do not play the same role in Islam that they do in Christianity. More critical are narratives that have been formulated in terms of legal traditions, what is more appropriately called Islamic philosophy and is frequently expressed in poetry. This leads the narratives to a more holistic focus on everyday life and instructions for living—what these believers are

---

[78]Ibid., 430. Interestingly, Islamist scholar and missionary J. Dudley Woodberry argues that Muhammad can be understood as a prophet calling the polytheist Arab tribes back to the worship of the one God. Woodberry, "Contextualization Among Muslims: Reusing Common Pillars," in *Understanding Insider Movements: Disciples of Jesus Within Diverse Religious Communities*, ed. Harley Talman and John Jay Travis (Pasadena, CA: William Carey Library, 2015), 415.

calling the "way of righteousness." Acoba illustrates this difference later in his article when he narrates an encounter between a missionary he calls Rick and a Muslim believer, Murad. Rick was feeling like a failure after many years of work among Muslim people when even those (like Murad) who had chosen to follow Christ avoided him. Acoba was able to mediate this dispute by pointing out that Murad was in fact deeply grateful for the goodness Rick had shown to him and his family but that he had gone his own way when Rick had not understood the way Murad felt it necessary to practice his faith.[79]

On the surface this expresses a classic tension between a missionary and native convert, but in this case I believe something deeper was going on. Two very different ways of understanding life and religion were being played out. Rick had a clear method to his ministry: converts had to attend Bible study, participate in contextual worship weekly, and attend discipleship training; that is, religious devotion had to be expressed in the typical categories and performed in the expected practices of Western Christianity. Murad felt these practices were inappropriate for a Muslim context. At the same time he had no doubt his Muslim identity was compatible with his commitment to *Isa al Masih*. Though he continued faithfully observing the Five Pillars of Islam, he was also persistent in sharing the good news of *Isa al Masih* with those around him, attracting others to this new way (including his wife). Rick could not disconnect the good news from the forms that he brought with him from the West; Murad, as Acoba notes, "merely wanted the simplicity of the power of the Good News to be lived out."[80] This difference is not simply about what Scripture calls believers to do and what another faith has proposed; it is fundamentally about two different notions of what religion looks like on the ground. Rick could not imagine a faith that did not issue from the intellectual understanding of Scripture as this is elaborated in study and reflection; the case of Murad recalls our discussion in an earlier chapter where Talal Asad described the Muslim understanding of faith and piety as these shape a particular form of life. Islamicist Abdur-Rahman Ibrahim Doi describes the difference:

> Since Islam does not subscribe to the idea that intellectual knowledge (illumination), however correctly imparted, would rightly lead the human will by itself,

[79]Acoba, "Towards an Understanding of Inclusivity," 438.
[80]Ibid., 441.

it insists that a Muslim should strive to increase his *taqwa* (piety) . . . by acquiring knowledge of the Quran . . . by performing devotional acts, and by reliance on God alone.[81]

While modern evangelicals like Rick might find such a program unappealing, a medieval Cistercian monk would recognize a similar structure to his spiritual journey, and it seemed natural to Murad.

Acoba gets at these fundamental differences by proposing that Rick was tied to religion as a source of structure and order, while Murad's aim was to celebrate the *event* of the gospel.[82] He goes on to describe the way faith is sparked and nurtured in this context by direct experience with the power of God, the *event* of God's presence in their lives. He recounts the story of a Christian leader's burial that was threatened by dark clouds (rain during a burial means the dead will not enter paradise). When they prayed, the clouds immediately moved away from the burial site, only to return as soon as the burial was over. Faith in this setting is one that emerges "along the way" in and through the events of everyday life in terms of the impermanence of this life. In the Muslim framework faith is to be lived out in daily life where Allah's blessings are experienced. But it is also a part of Muslim teaching that *Isa al Masih* will return at the end of history. And so all of life can be seen as a journey toward the completion of the kingdom. Meanwhile, these believers seek to express the event in new ways—you may recall how they were able to define the *da'wah* as inviting others to the way of righteousness—that grow out of their lived context.

Of particular significance is the way events of everyday life become theologically charged hermeneutical spaces that allowed for Scripture to shed new light. Their appreciation for community as "inclusively diverse" allowed them to appreciate the multiple spaces where Christian truth and Islamic practice could be brought together and new theological formulations—new *convivencia*—could be formed from the "local hermeneutical tools found in this

---

[81]Abdur-Rahman Ibrahim Doi, "Sunnism," in *Islamic Spirituality: Foundations*, ed. Seyyed Hossein Nasr (New York: Crossroad, 1987), 157-58.

[82]Acoba makes the suggestive proposal that this might be usefully put in conversation with the theology of the "event" proposed by John Caputo in *The Weakness of God: A Theology of the Event* (Bloomington: Indiana University Press, 2006). Acoba, "Towards an Understanding of Inclusivity," 440-41.

cultural space."[83] This diversity was proposed in opposition to the metanarrative the missionaries sought to impose, which in their view had served to
thwart the transformational power of the gospel. Meanwhile, the local conditions continued to provide, Acoba notes, the matrix and resources for their
discipleship. He insists, however, that they do not see this as contextualization
(which they firmly associate with evangelical missionaries); "rather they are
'naturally and genuinely' living out the teachings of *Isa al Masih* within the
framework of Islam. As Muslims, their Muslimhood has never changed."[84]

To celebrate the new thing that God may be doing in this place is not to
avoid facing the quandaries and tensions that remain. Acoba points out that
for many Magindanon followers of Christ the cross has become so inter-
twined with Christian appropriation of their land that it is no longer a symbol
of deliverance but a sign of oppression. Some participants even expressed their
hatred for the cross since it had been so intricately related to the Christians'
appropriation of their land. This dilemma recalls Elsa Tamez's description of
the struggle of the gods in Latin America. The challenge for these believers is
to see how the meaning of the cross has been subverted by these Christian
colonial practices and to recognize that Christ's suffering is better understood
as illuminating their own marginality and persecution.

Clearly this emergent community is finding its way through uncharted ter-
ritory. Not only do they come from different ethnic communities, each with
its own practices and traditions, but there are now three generations of believers whose experience reflects a rapidly changing world. As we have argued
throughout this book, the challenge facing the body of Christ today is to see
these differences as opportunities and resources and not only as problems.
Interestingly, the latest generation of Magindanon followers of *Isa al Masih* is
characterized by a new global awareness, alert to the potential of social net-
working. While an earlier generation thought of the kingdom of God in terms
of the *Ummah* (the worldwide community of Islam), the later generation's
conception of *da'wah* is bolder and more intentional in its sense of mission.[85]
All this suggests that the Spirit of God is at work empowering a new generation
of witnesses to the gospel.

---

[83]Acoba, "Towards an Understanding of Inclusivity," 417-18.
[84]Ibid., 426.
[85]Ibid., 428.

The diversity of contexts and believing communities that we have surveyed might seem disconcerting to one in search of a common denominator. Despite the differences, what seems consistent is the indication that the Spirit of God may be doing a new thing that calls Christians to listen carefully and to be willing to see fresh forms of believing communities. But it should not discourage us from raising questions about the implications of this for missions and for the growth of a global Christian community. It is to this learning and these questions that we turn in the final two chapters. In the next we ask what these movements might mean for our conception of mission today, and in the final chapter we will explore how we might think about the church in new ways.

CHAPTER FIVE

RELIGION AND THE
MISSION OF CHRIST

In the attempt to propose a theological framework for understanding the newer forms of insider and emergent mission, I have sought in earlier chapters to make two fundamental points. First, in chapter two I emphasized that creation and renewal represent God's primary and ongoing work and that the formation of culture and religion is always to be seen, in part, as a human response to this work and this presence. Second, because of this, although culture and religion are human work, God has a continuing stake in both, and in them, as Scripture says, God is not left without a witness—in and through them God seeks to work out the renewal of all things. The third chapter developed this second claim by reviewing the way religion is portrayed in the biblical narrative and showing that, because religion reflects the human longing and search for God, God's attitude toward religion changed to reflect not only God's ongoing re-creative work but the changing historical situations of this human response. All through Scripture and human history, God is not indifferent to the cry of the human heart, whatever the circumstances surrounding that cry. The previous chapter of case studies in various ways confirmed both the renewing presence of God in these other faiths and, at the same time, the centrality of the work of Christ in transforming communities and cultures.

In this chapter we turn more directly to ask how, in the light of Christ's command to make disciples of all the peoples, followers of Christ are to understand and engage the variety of religions and the obvious working of God's Spirit in these places. This will involve in large part seeking to clarify what religion is and how it functions in people's lives. To do this we return to the disparity between Western and non-Western views of religion and illustrate this difference by comparing Christian and Muslim notions of worship. Finally, we will want to ask, in the light of these intractable differences, how mission may be reconceived to better relate and promote God's transforming work.

As we have seen, in his address on Mars Hill Paul stressed that God had allotted to each people group times and spaces, "so that they would search for God and perhaps grope for him and find him" (Acts 17:27). Religion, then, in its basic sense represents the practices associated with the human search for God, and the times and spaces they employ in this search. I have called these particular places and times hermeneutical spaces, and I want to develop this notion in more detail in this chapter. I find it telling that Paul should underline that God allotted to people places and times because this puts forward an essential dimension of all religions. That is, they grow out of and express the texture and feel of places people call home. This was evident in all the case studies we reviewed in the last chapter.

One of the problems associated with recent Western views of religions, as we have seen, is that they have become radically disconnected from any sense of place. Thus we have lost sight of the deep rootedness of religions in their cultural and historical situations and their contingent and fluid character. This is a result, among other factors, of the developments since the Reformation that we traced briefly in the first chapter, and which I want to explore further here. This abstraction of religion from any particular setting has become so normal, especially for Protestants, that we do not see in the long history of humanity and even among the varieties of Christianities how unusual this is. I want to argue that this myopia keeps Western Protestant Christians from properly understanding how religion actually functions in people's lives. This not only results in the failure to appreciate what insider movements might portend but also imposes a serious limitation on what the mission of God may be today.

Let me linger a bit on the view of religion that I am developing and tease out its significance for my argument. I am using *religion* in the general sense of the particular cultural practices that develop to express the inbuilt human longing for God—the spaces humans construct to look for and even find God. As I have noted, the idea of religion as a separate sphere of life is a product of modernity and, for many people, simply incomprehensible. As Karen

Armstrong points out, the idea of religion as codified and personal was entirely absent in the great civilizations, from ancient Greece through Mesopotamia to India. Religion expressed a much more general sense of how life should be lived and the specific practices that embodied that life. In the Greco-Roman world, to call a cultic observance or the keeping of an oath *religio* meant that it was simply incumbent on one—something that one must do as a member of that particular social group.[1]

In the modern period, as a result of changes brought about by the Reformation and as these were worked out in the Enlightenment, religion has taken on a particular profile that it had never previously exhibited (and that is still strange to most people outside the West).[2] As we saw in the first chapter, after the Reformation and Enlightenment religion was no longer something to be done but (primarily) something to be believed. Moreover, religion was seen no longer as an aspect of the whole of life but as something that stands in a separate category, alongside economics, politics, and so on (from which many assume it must be kept separate). Naturally we tend to assume that religion everywhere functions, or should function, in the same way that it does in the West. The result has been the tendency to essentialize religion as a homogenous concept that retains its identity across space and time. One can easily see that this violates the fundamental nature of religious longing as it is tied to particular places and times, and to the cultures of those places, therefore differing widely and changing dramatically over time. To speak then of Hinduism or Buddhism as an abstract concept makes little sense and contributes nothing to understanding what these religions might mean for a Christian mission. As H. L. Richard notes, they are empty concepts.[3]

In his study of theology and race Willie Jennings, whom we met earlier, has described how even the dominant Western understanding of theology has been deeply influenced by the displacement that has characterized the spread of Christianity. Not only have Christians, both Catholic and Protestant,

---

[1]Karen Armstrong, *Fields of Blood: Religion and the History of Violence* (New York: Knopf, 2014), 4-5.

[2]However, Juergensmeyer points out that this process of institutionalization, which hardens lines of influence and polices the border areas, has been characteristic of all religions at various times. Mark Juergensmeyer, "Introduction," in *The Oxford Handbook of Global Religion*, ed. Mark Juergensmeyer (New York: Oxford University Press, 2006), 8.

[3]H. L. Richard, "Religious Syncretism as a Syncretistic Concept: The Inadequacy of the 'World Religions' Paradigm," in *Understanding Insider Movements: Disciples of Jesus Within Diverse Religious Communities*, ed. Harley Talman and John Jay Travis (Pasadena, CA: William Carey Library, 2015), 343.

abstracted their understanding of the gospel from any particular place—consider how mainstream theological texts seldom reflect any particular geography or even any particular ethnic perspective, or, what is worse, Jennings notes, the extension of Christianity in the missionary movement—they actually succeeded in *displacing* people from their various geographical contexts. The process of conversion to Christ was mostly presented as a kind of creation ex nihilo and thus an extraction from the believer's setting. Here is how Jennings describes the results in the mission to Latin America:

> Detached from the land, oblivious to the ongoing decimation of native ecologies, deeply suspicious of native religious practices, and most important, enclosed within Iberian whiteness, the performance of Christian theology would produce a new, deformed, and deforming intellectual circuit.[4]

The reference to race here is relevant in that displacement from native contexts involved at the same time undermining the identities that were connected with those places. This process also characterized the settlement and evangelization of North America. For Native Americans, connection with the land is essential to their identity.[5] Vine Deloria Jr., a Native American leader, believes white American identities have been indeterminate because they have not learned from the inhabitants of the place where they live.

> The indeterminacy of American identities stems, in part, from the nation's inability to deal with the Indian people. Americans wanted to feel a natural affinity with the continent, and it was the Indians who could teach them such aboriginal closeness. Yet, in order to control the landscape they had to destroy the original inhabitants.[6]

This sad project resulted, in large part, from the fact that the significance of place had been eliminated from European immigrants' understanding of religion. And this weakness certainly accounts for a portion of the dismay that many Christians show toward insider movements.

Throughout history, because of this rootedness, religions have frequently appeared to outsiders as ad hoc and idiosyncratic affairs. But their historical character also allowed religions to have permeable and changing boundaries,

---

[4]Willie James Jennings, *The Christian Imagination: Theology and the Origins of Race* (New Haven, CT: Yale University Press, 2010), 81-82.
[5]Ibid., 79.
[6]Vine Deloria, *Playing Indian* (New Haven, CT: Yale University Press, 1998), 5, quoted in Jennings, *Christian Imagination*, 41.

pushing them to expand into new territories or contract during times of decay, and allowing them to interact with, learn from, and influence neighboring faiths. We see this in Confucian and Taoist influences on Buddhism in China, in Muslim influences on Christianity in medieval Europe, and as a part of the rise of the Indo-Islamic civilization in thirteenth to fifteenth-century India, which was a remarkably creative synthesis of Muslim and Hindu elements. One concrete example of the borrowing this facilitated is the familiar rosary that Catholics use in their prayer. Evidence links this to Muslim prayer beads in the Middle Ages, a practice that in turn was probably influenced by Buddhist prayer beads in Central Asia.[7]

This leads me to the question I want to pose in this chapter: what if we thought of religion, or religions, including Christianity, not as fixed entities with clearly defined borders but as fluid spaces that reflect particular cultural situations, where people have developed various ways of responding to God (or gods or the spirits)? Further, what if we understood those spaces as places where people are working out the possible meaning of God's presence there, "so that they would search for God and perhaps grope for him and find him" (Acts 17:27), as Paul puts it—that is, as hermeneutical spaces where people are not only open to God's voice but also prepared (by the Spirit) for that word?

What then if we understood mission to be the activity of witnessing to the re-creative work of God, centering on Jesus' death and resurrection and on the pouring out of the Holy Spirit on all flesh, but amid these diverse expressions of the human search for God, whereby the stories people tell about themselves and the spirits can potentially be incorporated into the narrative of the Christian gospel? Or, better, what if mission represented ways in which the Christian story might be inscribed on these stories, much like Dante in his *Commedia* inscribed the pilgrimage to God in Christ on the myths of the classical world?

REIMAGINING RELIGION

It is critical for understanding Christian mission that it be recognized that religion for most people is an expression of identity tied to the traditions of a particular place, and often expressed in stories, legends, aesthetic artifacts, and rituals. My whole project in this book includes calling for a more holistic

---

[7]See on this Juergensmeyer, "Introduction," 4-8. He notes also the influence of Greek ideas of logos or Zoroastrian notions of the devil and heaven on Christianity.

understanding of religion that includes all these dimensions. If this holistic understanding is appropriate, so I argue, wherever the gospel goes, if it will be understood at all, it must first be framed in terms of the imaginative logic and the social and aesthetic patterns that make that place into a home. If you want to understand Appalachian Christianity, you must know something about bluegrass music; if you want to know about the Muslim religion in Java, you must study Wayang Kulit drama; and so on. And if it is true that religion represents the core both of people's identities and of their sense of place, then, in the first instance at least, the news about God's love in Christ must be framed in terms of that religion—that is, in terms of the search after God by which they frame their identity.

Scholars of religion today have begun to recognize the varieties of religious expression and the multiple ways in which religion comes to expression. Catherine Albanese, for example, in her influential textbook on American religion, has argued that religion consists of four dimensions: explanations of meaning (or creeds), rules that govern behavior (or codes), social institutions (churches, mosques, etc.), and multisensory communal rituals that engage believers' bodies (what she calls cultuses).[8] According to this contemporary definition, religion consists of the multiple ways in which people *make sense* of their lives and the world they know.

The way religion involves many interrelated aspects of life was also emphasized in the classic definition of religion by Clifford Geertz, which, as we noted in the first chapter, has been so influential on contemporary missiology. He argued that religion is best understood as a "system of symbols," which, as he puts it, formulated "conceptions of a general order of existence and cloth[ed] these *conceptions* with such an aura of factuality that the moods and motivations seem uniquely realistic."[9] But, as noted earlier, this definition has been subject to critique by Talal Asad and others as reflecting a Western and particularly Protestant reading of religion.[10] Notice that in focusing on

---

[8]Catherine L. Albanese, *America: Religions and Religion*, 3rd ed. (Belmont, CA: Wadsworth, 1999), 8-10.

[9]Clifford Geertz, "Religion as a Cultural System," in *The Interpretation of Cultures: Selected Essays* (New York: Basic Books, 1973), 90, emphasis added.

[10]One could argue that Albanese's definition similarly reflects her American setting, though she has sought to come to a more universal view, in particular by adding the fourth (ritual) dimension in more recent editions of her influential text.

"*conceptions* of a general order of existence," Geertz emphasizes the ways people make sense of their lives. The default focus, in other words, falls on what Albanese calls creeds—on "making sense" of life. The rituals that express these conceptions merely serve as "clothing" for these conceptions. This is not wrong of course, but it is a peculiarly Protestant reading of religion, as we described this in the first chapter. But, as I will note below, for Muslims ritual practice is of the essence of their faith, and theological descriptions of meaning, when they exist, are relatively less important. It is not accidental that those voicing this critique of Geertz (like Asad and Saba Mahmood) have been students of Islam, for whom the dimensions of religion marginalized during the Reformation are central.

Sociologists of religion are increasingly recognizing the complex and interrelated nature of belief and practice. Mark Chaves, in his fine study of American congregations, has attempted to move beyond Geertz in his understanding of religion. Chaves registers his desire to approach congregations in terms of "specific sets of practices" rather than in terms of the dominant neoclassical approach of all-encompassing symbolic universes.[11] His approach, which he terms "ecological," is a helpful attempt to understand the embodied and emplaced character of religion.

But what most studies of religion in the West overlook, including Chaves, is the role of longstanding religious traditions, many stretching over many centuries, in forming religious practices and the accompanying imagination. Consider a recent definition of religion offered by Ann Taves: Religion is "the process whereby people decide on the meaning of events and decide what matters most."[12] While this fits well with the ethnographic turn to the subject that we have described, it fails to illumine how religious practices are authorized over time, and it still promotes the notion that religion involves the unattached individual evaluating and constructing the religious self. Again, this view is not mistaken, but it is parochial. It reflects a modern, and Western, understanding of persons and community—that communities are formed by

---

[11]Mark Chaves, *Congregations in America* (Cambridge, MA: Harvard University Press, 2004), 10.

[12]Ann Taves, "'Religion' in the Humanities and the Humanities in the University," *Journal of the American Academy of Religion* 79, no. 2 (2011): 291. She wants to avoid "stipulated definitions" of religion that don't leave the defining of religion to the actors themselves. See also Ann Taves, *Religious Experience Reconsidered: A Building-Block Approach to the Study of Religion and Other Special Things* (Princeton, NJ: Princeton University Press, 2009).

a collection of selves who freely choose to belong or not. And it also displays a peculiarly American understanding of religion as a personal construction. But for many people religious patterns of practice take shape over time and create communal disciplines that both form communities and foster religious identities. And these identities reflect widely different and diverse forms of life that call for careful discernment.

My goal in this discussion of the nature of religion is not to suggest that the Western view is mistaken, or that the Muslim view is somehow privileged, but to recognize the fundamental differences in these approaches. Further, in recognizing these differences, I want to point out the ways that the Western assumptions about religion have infected the missionary movement and impeded the ability to see and learn from how God might be working in fresh ways today.

RELIGION AS A CULTURALLY EMBEDDED RESPONSE TO THE PRESENCE OF GOD

Let me attempt then to define elements of a more comprehensive view of religion that allows for these differences and that will provide a possible framework for our approach to insider and emergent movements. In the course of my own recent research in Christian, Buddhist, and Muslim communities in Los Angeles, three elements emerged as constitutive of the three religions I studied: cognitive representation, ritual practice, and spatial/visual settings and cues.[13] The first refers to the role that verbal formulations—creeds, Scriptural readings, or confessions—play in religious practice. The second points to physical, embodied practices that people perform individually or in communal settings—standing, sitting, crossing themselves, and so on. The third highlights the spatial setting, the place, where people gather and the visual (and oral) textures displayed there, especially as these reflect inherited cultural values. These three elements, functioning in integrated ways, together mark devotional practices that people find satisfying and often aesthetically pleasing.[14] To these, Albanese adds codes, which may be better

---

[13]Research conducted on Christianity, Buddhism, and Islam from 2009 to 2012 and funded by the Henry Luce Foundation, published as William A. Dyrness, *Senses of Devotion: Interfaith Aesthetics in Buddhist and Muslim Communities* (Eugene, OR: Cascade, 2013).

[14]I have been influenced by the work of Tanya Luhrmann. See T. M. Luhrmann, Howard Nusbaum, and Ronald Thisted, "The Absorption Hypothesis: Learning to Hear God in Evangelical Christianity," *American Anthropologist* 112, no. 1 (2010): 67-68, where they develop notions of interpretation

expressed in terms of particular moral sensitivities since many religions do not codify specified behavior.

These three (or four) elements are always present in religious practice: all great religious traditions have sacred texts, they specify particular ritual acts, and all have spatial (even geographical) orientation and artifacts and particular moral sensitivities,[15] but what distinguishes different religious traditions is the relative weight given to one element over against another. This is where we Protestants have to be reminded of the beam in our eye represented by our own religious preferences. We, for example, tend to harbor a deep suspicion of ritual—which we are tempted to dismiss as something done to earn God's favor. On the other hand, we take for granted that verbal elements should predominate since these are facilitated by both the teachings and the sung prayers that make up such an important part of contemporary worship. Indeed, in many ways such intellectual components *constitute* the Protestant worship experience: when we have heard a good sermon on a great biblical passage, we go home satisfied. And so when we enter into dialogue with practitioners of other traditions, we naturally ask these others what they "believe" about this or that, or we might want to compare the "teaching" of our different religious texts. But this invariably puts these friends at a disadvantage because what they believe is often not as important as ritual practices, which we Protestants have already set aside. Indeed, what they believe may not matter at all. As several Buddhist respondents noted, Buddhist belief is very thin; meditative disciplines are far more constitutive of religious formation. Similarly for still other traditions, various practices or visual elements that believers find deeply satisfying may take priority over the cognitive forms. Think of the role icons play in Eastern Orthodoxy.

But for Protestant Christians, ritual practices, if they matter at all, must have particular symbolic content; that is, they must refer back to the verbal formulations (cf. Geertz). By contrast, performance of the daily prayers for the Muslim resists symbolic reference. Again, though one element or another may predominate, all are part of religious devotion. Protestants of course do

---

(cognitive representation) and practice. These assumptions are developed in Luhrmann's more recent *When God Talks Back: Understanding the American Evangelical Relationship with God* (New York: Knopf, 2012).

[15] I don't mean to imply that this list is exclusive. There may be other elements that are equally basic, but these are typically present in the three religions I have studied.

perform certain things, and they *shape* the places where they worship even if they give little thought to these, though such things are not as important as sermons and Bible readings. This is why so many Protestants feel no handicap in meeting for worship in theater-like settings or even in storefronts. By contrast, Eastern Orthodox believers give careful thought to the construction of their spaces and the elaborate icons that fill those spaces. These are considered essential to their experience of prayer.[16] Notice, however, for all religious traditions these various elements and their relationships are all theory laden; that is, the inclination to emphasize one or another element is deeply shaped by the disciplinary matrix, including assumptions and patterns of practice developed over long periods of time by that tradition. Moreover, and equally significant for my argument, these patterns inevitably become part of the deep structure of the cultures of these places and the identities of people living there.

THE RELIGION OF ISLAM AND CHRISTIAN MISSIONS

To illustrate these differences, let me provide a comparative case study. Since Islam is the most prominent site of insider practice, let me compare typical Muslim attitudes toward worship with our usual Christian understandings. Not only may this illumine for us the way interfaith understanding is enabled by careful comparative study, but it may also illumine the possible ways God may be at work in other religions.

Islam, while it often appears strange to modern Western Christians, shares an important slice of its history with earlier forms of Christianity. Muhammad can be seen not only as a reformer of the rampant polytheism of seventh-century Arabia but also as someone who was deeply familiar with Jewish and Christian practices—he called these neighbors "people of the book."[17] Dudley Woodberry has shown that the practices of Islam, what are called the Five Pillars of their faith, were previously the possession of Jews and Christians.[18] The Qur'an itself reflects at many points the influence of the Christian

---

[16]I explored the differences among the Christian traditions in an earlier study: William A. Dyrness, *Senses of the Soul: Art and the Visual in Christian Worship* (Eugene, OR: Cascade, 2009).

[17]See Karen Armstrong, *Muhammad: A Prophet for Our Time* (San Francisco: HarperCollins, 2006). It is evident, however, that his exposure to Christianity was to a variety of (often deviant) forms.

[18]J. Dudley Woodberry, "Contextualization Among Muslims: Reusing Common Pillars," in *Understanding Insider Movements: Disciples of Jesus Within Diverse Religious Communities*, ed. Harley Talman and John Jay Travis (Pasadena, CA: William Carey Library, 2015), 407-35. He shows the dependency in great detail in order to argue that believers in Christ now reusing these practices

and Jewish Scriptures. Indeed, scholars have called it a kind of Arabic lectionary of the Bible, not unlike the Jewish Targums. All of this suggests that Muhammad may have, initially, considered his role to be that of continuing the previous Judeo-Christian tradition.[19]

The mutual dependency does not stop with the early history of Islam. The rise of medieval culture in Europe would have been impossible apart from the influence and cultural wisdom of Moorish Spain, which reached its apogee in the eighth and ninth centuries.[20] We have seen earlier how similar are Muslim and medieval Christian (especially monastic) practices, where, for example, non-memorial prayer within a communal setting in both is understood to be spiritually formational. Even Muslim understandings of faith resonate with biblical teaching. As Talal Asad notes, the Arabic word *iman*, usually translated "faith," doesn't carry the epistemological connotations of the English word. "It is better translated as the virtue of faithfulness toward God, an unquestioning habit of obedience that God requires of those faithful to him."[21] Similarly *taqwa* (which may be translated as "piety") suggests both an inward disposition and "a manner of practical conduct."[22] But, as we have seen, the effacement of the medieval spiritual traditions at the Reformation has led modern Christians to perceive Christianity in ways that radically diverge from Islam—and indeed from their own Christian past.[23] Further reflection on these similarities, and the current differences, may then be a useful exercise.

To further elaborate this comparison, consider this contemporary description

---

are in many ways simply taking back what originally belonged to them.

[19]This is the argument of Martin Accad in "Christian Attitudes Toward Islam and Muslims: A Kerygmatic Approach," in Talman and Travis, *Understanding Insider Movements*, 437-53. Accad thinks that Muhammad may have changed his attitude when (and because) the Jews rejected this continuity. This article also describes the intricate relationship between the Qur'an and the Bible.

[20]See María Rosa Menocal, *The Ornament of the World: How Muslims, Jews, and Christians Created a Culture of Tolerance in Medieval Spain* (Boston: Little, Brown, 2002). For a good summary of the early history of Islam, see Samuel H. Moffett, *A History of Christianity in Asia*, vol. 1 (San Francisco: Harper, 1992).

[21]Talal Asad, *Formations of the Secular: Christianity, Islam and Modernity* (Palo Alto, CA: Stanford University Press, 2003), 90. This again may be due to the fact that Muhammad himself was influenced by the Christian (and Jewish) piety that he observed around him. See A. Scott Moreau, *Contextualization in World Missions: Mapping and Assessing Evangelical Models* (Grand Rapids: Kregel, 2012), 159, and the literature cited there.

[22]Saba Mahmood, *Politics of Piety; The Islamic Revival and the Feminist Subject* (Princeton, NJ: Princeton University Press, 2005), 4n7.

[23]I believe in most cases this was not the intent of the magisterial reformers, especially Luther, but it is the effect that this convulsive period in many cases has had on subsequent religious practice.

of Islam offered by the work of Saba Mahmood, who writes on the general revival of Islamic spirituality since the 1970s.[24] She proposes that the practice of Islam is best understood as a "discursive formation," in that it provides "the very ground through which the subjectivities and self-understanding of a tradition's adherents are constituted." Specifically, she argues that this consists of elements that closely follow the three elements of religion that I stressed earlier. This discursive formation provides (1) a mode of engagement with sacred texts, by which it (2) creates certain embodied capacities, what I have called ritual practices, which in turn (3) shape sensibilities that issue in various artifacts and buildings.[25]

Muslim believers live out of a story line that overlaps significantly with the Christian story, moving from creation through to consummation and the last judgment. But the embodiment of this story in Muslim worship is significantly different. Unlike our Western conceptions, religion is not separable from other parts of life; *din*, the Arabic word for "religion," refers to a whole way of life. In their worship *din* is represented in the oral recitation of the Qur'an and embodied in the visual calligraphy of verses of the Qur'an on walls of the mosque, as well as in the practices of ablution and prayer. Their prayer, Muslims believe, is a response to the actual presence of God in the words they hear and see— represented most clearly in the call to prayer. Specifically, Islam (lit. "submission") calls believers to observe the Five Pillars: confession of faith (*shahadah*): "There is no God but Allah, and Muhammad is his prophet"; five daily prayers and prayers at the mosque with their attendant rituals of cleansing (*salat*, pl. *salawat*); pilgrimage to Mecca once in a lifetime (*hajj*); fasting, especially during the month of Ramadan; and, finally, almsgiving (*zakat*). All of these are meant to exemplify submission to God. In my research I found that these practices provide Muslim believers concrete spaces and occasions for the development of the virtuous self, which has led me to suggest that Islam can be understood as a kind of spiritual architecture that structures believers' lives and gives them a sense of order and direction.[26]

Mahmood, in her book, studies in depth contemporary women's groups in Cairo, Egypt, where women gather together (often with women leaders) in large numbers to pray together in the mosque. She argues that faithful

---

[24]Mahmood, *Politics of Piety*, 114-17.
[25]Ibid., 115.
[26]This is developed further in Dyrness, *Senses of Devotion*, 67-99.

performance of ritual prayer (*salat*), for example, does not indicate submission to a male-dominated politics or a loss of a woman's own subjectivity. But neither did their practice constitute a search for individual fulfillment as feminist scholars would understand this in the West. Rather, the goal of these women of "being close to God," she discovered, involved a complex disciplinary program in which virtues are developed and expressed in the communal performance of their ritual prayers. The intention to follow God entailed a prescribed sequence of gestures, words, and attitudes. These women, Mahmood argued, developed their sense of self in the performance of these practices. She summarizes this process by saying,

> The *work* bodily practices perform in crafting a subject—rather than the *meanings* they signify—carries the analytic weight. In other words the "how" of the practices is explored rather than their symbolic or hermeneutical value.[27]

Note that the value these women attached to these practices resided not in the theological meanings behind these practices, as they would for Christians, but in the actual performance of these ritual prayers—much as centering prayer in the medieval monasteries served to move monks toward union with God. Mahmood describes why one woman she calls Mona was able to get up for the early prayers and what difference this made in her day.

> *Salat* is not just what you say with your mouth and what you do with your limbs. It is a state of your heart. So when you do things in a day for God and avoid other things because of Him, it means you're thinking of Him, and therefore it becomes easy for you to strive for Him against yourself and your desires. If you correct these issues, you will be able to rise up for the morning prayer as well.[28]

Mona's identity as a Muslim and her sense of self are both developed in the performance of these prayers.

While similar in many ways to medieval contemplative practice (which is experiencing a revival even among evangelical Protestants), Muslim worship is radically different from the contemporary Christian understanding of worship. First of all, Christian worship as this has developed among Western evangelicals centers on drawing out the meaning and implications of what we have

---

[27]Mahmood, *Politics of Piety*, 122, emphasis original.
[28]Ibid., 125.

called "the gospel" for a personal experience of faith.[29] In many churches the congregation recites a creed, Scripture is read, and sermons are preached. I found in my research that when Protestants were asked what was central to worship, the answer invariably involved some form of the "story" of the gospel, usually embodied in the sermon or the "teaching." Consider this response by a pastor in Long Beach, California, expressing what should be central to worship:

> There are a variety of elements that we do in [the service] to engage people in this overarching story that we really try to emphasize here. It's not the worship. It's the story that prompts the worship . . . and that's an . . . important distinction, because . . . I think that so much about these worship wars is that we're fighting about worship. . . . We need to change the scope of the argument. That if we were about the story, [we would see] that it's really much larger than us, that worship is prompted by the story.[30]

This means that other ritual and visual elements must be oriented to the meaning expressed in this story—they must always be symbolic, or referential, in this narrow sense.

But equally important to true worship for Christians is the need to personally appropriate this story, to experience the presence of God in a deep and personal way. One of our respondents, José, described the process of worship in this way: "The process of starting with praise and then . . . if the conditions are right [and] the Holy Spirit is there, with the talent of the worship leader [and] the ambiance, my frame of mind, of being able to really enter into worship and adoration. That's for me the goal, and sometimes that happens— it doesn't always happen." The Holy Spirit uses elements of the worship experience to "spark," that is, to allow believers to experience the presence of God.[31]

This experience of worship—focusing on the cognitive meaning that is personally appropriated—constitutes worship that many evangelical Protestants, including the present author, find satisfying and fulfilling. Worshipers from this tradition assume that these practices best reflect the intention of Scripture, and they are not wrong about this. But they may not recognize ways in which

---

[29]This of course is to generalize a complex reality, but I am using conclusions that I have drawn from my own ethnographic research among contemporary Protestants in Southern California. See Dyrness, *Senses of the Soul* (2009) and *Senses of Devotion* (2013).

[30]Quoted in Dyrness, *Senses of Devotion*, 106.

[31]Ibid., 106-7.

they also reflect particular cultural values that have developed over time—those values and attitudes stemming from the Reformation (seasoned by the Enlightenment and the Romantic movement) that we reviewed briefly in the first chapter. For example, our emphasis on the personal and inward appropriation of Christ's presence reflects, in addition to biblical teaching, particular streams of medieval mysticism as these were influential on later pietism and the evangelical revivals. These streams were in turn deeply influential on the Romanticism of the nineteenth century that has so profoundly marked contemporary spirituality.[32]

So a close analysis of the rise and influence of our evangelical practices makes clear that Christian worship of this kind *represents an appropriation by a particular stream of the Christian tradition of early modern (and later Enlightenment and Romantic) sensitivities.* This tradition represents, I would argue, an important interpretation of the work of Christ that allows it to be heard in a modern Western setting; it is a critical hermeneutical space. But in terms of the broader Christian tradition, even in terms of biblical teaching, it is not necessarily privileged—even if, for its practitioners, it is a more transparent and satisfying expression of the gospel than any other. It does not represent the full meaning of religion, nor does it exhaust the possibilities inherent in the gospel.[33] Moreover, sensitive listening to Muslim believers discloses practices that, though different from those typical to Christians, issues in experiences that we might characterize as life giving, even if they are not salvific. But if this is so, we might venture to reframe the question raised earlier: might it be possible for other practices, developed in vastly different settings, to be carriers of genuine faith in Christ? In fact, the case study from Mindanao in the last chapter provides an example of just such an emergent form.

DO CHRISTIANS AND MUSLIMS (AND JEWS) WORSHIP THE SAME GOD?

But there is one concern left hanging in our discussion of Islam: there are some who would argue emphatically that we Christians and Muslims do not address

---

[32]The most important scholar to make this connection in our generation is Charles Taylor; see Taylor, *Sources of the Self: The Making of the Modern Identity* (Cambridge, MA: Harvard University Press, 1989) and *A Secular Age* (Cambridge, MA: Harvard University Press, 2007).

[33]In fact, Karen Armstrong writes, "The only faith tradition that does fit the modern notion of religion as something codified and private is Protestant Christianity, which, like *religion* in this sense of the word, is also a product of the early modern period." Armstrong, *Fields of Blood*, 5.

or worship the same God. This question has received new attention in connection with Muslim attempts in Malaysia to forbid Christians from even using the name *Allah* since, in their minds, the Christian trinitarian God is clearly a different God—despite the fact that Arabic-speaking Christians in the Middle East used *Allah* for God long before the appearance of Muhammad.[34] Many religious traditions don't believe in a personal God, or a single God, and so the question may be framed differently. But especially in the case of the three Abrahamic faiths, contemporary theologians have begun to ask whether it is possible to think of all three faiths as worshiping the same God. This question was recently addressed by a group of Christian, Jewish, and Muslim scholars.[35]

On such a disputed question one should not expect consensus, but many have argued that according to the testimony of most believers it seems clear that they *intend* the same God. Muslim scholar Reza Shah-Kazemi argues that the same God is sought, at least with respect to the that-ness if not the what-ness—which is conceived by human intellect.[36] Jewish writer Peter Ochs believes that the same God is worshiped, though "by way of mutually exclusive practices of worship."[37] Presbyterian scholar Amy Plantinga Pauw noted that all confess God as creator of heaven and earth and that by their own admission there can be only one such creator; thus they confess the one creator God.[38] More importantly, as Catholic scholar Denys Turner argues on Christian grounds, any real knowledge of God is received by grace, and so we might assume that whatever is known of God in other religions is similarly received rather than constructed.[39] This last assertion recalls theologians' claims we have reviewed, that the universal awareness of God in the human heart is itself evidence of God's grace.

But what about the troublesome Christian conviction about the Trinity: that the God Christians worship is both one and three? Interestingly, both

---

[34]See on this the J. Dudley Woodberry article, "Contextualization Among Muslims: Reusing Common Pillars," 407-35.

[35]See Miroslav Volf, ed., *Do We Worship the Same God? Jews, Christians and Muslims in Dialogue* (Grand Rapids: Eerdmans, 2012). See also Miroslav Volf, *Allah: A Christian Response* (New York: HarperOne, 2011).

[36]Reza Shah-Kazemi, "Do Muslims and Christians Believe in the Same God?," in Volf, *Do We Worship the Same God?*, 78.

[37]Peter Ochs, "Do We Worship the Same God?," in Volf, *Do We Worship the Same God?*, 149.

[38]Amy Plantinga Pauw, "The Same God?," in Volf, *Do We Worship the Same God?*, 39.

[39]Denys Turner, "Christians, Muslims, and the Name of God: Who Owns It, and How Would We Know?," in Volf, *Do We Worship the Same God?*, 34.

Muslim and Jewish writers point out that their traditions contain resources that might allow for fruitful conversation on even this point. Specifically, Jewish scholar Alon Goshen-Gottstein, in a way that resonates with the argument of Daniel Boyarin, calls attention to the diversity of rabbinic notions of God, arguing that perhaps it is the loss of ritual and the fraught history of Christian-Jewish relations that have kept Judaism from recognizing Christianity as a legitimate expression of Judaism. He writes:

> Had the faith of Christianity remained true to classical Jewish ritual expression, there would have been little question as to the identity of God being worshiped through this ritual, even if a particular understanding of this God characterized a specific community of believers. Historical research suggests a far greater diversity in the understanding of the one God in late antiquity than is often recognized. Christian understanding could have conceivably developed as one form of Jewish understanding.[40]

Several have pointed out that all believers, whether Christians, Muslims, or Jews, are ultimately on the way to God, and all conceptions fall short of the reality they reference. Denys Turner put the matter this way: "Short of the beatific vision the whole story does not lie within our pre-mortem power to tell." Clearly, Turner avers, "all our secular criteria for identity are disabled regarding God." So even if, as several scholars have admitted, it would be difficult to know with certainty that we worship the same God, we can all join in the desire to know this God and to tell the full story of paradise. Indeed, Turner quips, "being able to tell [the full story] *is* paradise."[41] Amy Plantinga Pauw pushes this point further. In our journey to God we have come to see how dynamic, changing, and interdependent religious traditions are, which, by the grace of God, motivates us to listen and learn from one another as has often happened in the long history of interfaith encounters.[42]

Not all evangelicals will agree with such positive assessments, and this debate received renewed attention when Professor Larycia Hawkins was placed on administrative leave in late 2015 by Wheaton College for affirming (and quoting Pope Francis) that Christians and Muslims do worship the same God. Her position finds support in an article by Jesse Wheeler, who offers

[40]Alon Goshen-Gottstein, "Is It the Same God?," in Volf, *Do We Worship the Same God?*, 63.
[41]Turner, "Christians, Muslims, and the Name of God," 34-35.
[42]Plantinga Pauw, "The Same God?," 48.

historical and biblical evidence, centering on the loving character of Jesus himself, for assuming we worship the same God.[43] Timothy Tennent represents the more conservative position. While acknowledging an overlap between Allah and the Christian God, he has concluded that Allah is not the same as the Christian Father of Jesus.[44] The conviction that Christians focus their worship on God as manifested in Jesus Christ is of course a core Christian commitment. As Rowan Williams expresses this, we only have knowledge of God because of the particularity of Jesus. "What is to be said of God is that Jesus of Nazareth was born, ministered . . . died in such a way, and was raised from the dead."[45] Our case studies have made it clear that commitment to Christ lies at the center of the faith of these emerging communities. And just as the people of the early church began their reflection on the trinitarian nature of God by their experience of the Holy Spirit's power and through their worship of Jesus as God, so these believers are having their lives and religious convictions redrawn by their own experience with Christ.

In spite of our different conceptions about the creator God, the question still remains: How and when is this "difference" to be understood and evoked? How can this encounter prove to be a hermeneutical space in which both parties are transformed—a *convivencia* that allows for the liberating work of the Holy Spirit? This constitutes the core question I will address in the concluding chapter.

GOD'S PRESENCE IN RELIGION AND IN THE GOSPEL: CONTINUITY AND DISCONTINUITY

I have argued that religion represents both the search for God on the part of people in a particular place and time and also, theologically, the presence and calling of God in that place. I want to develop this theological point further here.

Up to this point the present chapter has focused largely on one side of the hermeneutical space of various forms of religion. These spaces provide, so I am arguing, places for practitioners to respond to and attempt to comprehend their encounter with God (or gods or the spirits)—where they grope after

[43]Jesse S. Wheeler, "'Is Allah God?': Five Reasons I Am Convinced," in Talman and Travis, *Understanding Insider Movements*, 517-19.
[44]Timothy C. Tennent, *Theology in the Context of World Christianity: How the Global Church Is Influencing the Way We Think About and Discuss Theology* (Grand Rapids: Zondervan, 2007), 36-37.
[45]Rowan Williams, *On Christian Theology* (New York: Blackwell, 2000), 156.

God. But there is another equally important aspect to these spaces: they are places where God is also present and active. It is not only the case that people naturally desire God; God in that very desire is also reaching toward them (see Jas 4:5).

Theologians from many traditions have long recognized the fact that God has placed within all people, because of their creation in God's image, a desire to know and find their final home in God, even if they have described this quest in different ways. Moreover, they have argued that this "desire" and the practices it elicits represent a place where God is also present. Augustine, the fifth-century Bishop of Hippo, argued famously in his *Confessions* that humans are made to search for God, and their hearts are restless until they find their rest in God. That classic autobiography is the testimony of Augustine's own search for and discovery of God.[46] During the Reformation, John Calvin claimed that a sense of God has been implanted within every human soul. As he wrote in the *Institutes*, "There is within the human mind, and indeed by natural instinct, an awareness of divinity. This we take to be beyond controversy. . . . God himself has implanted in all men a certain understanding of his divine majesty."[47] More than two centuries later John Wesley, in one of his later sermons on salvation, laid out an even more expansive view:

> If we take [salvation] in its utmost extent, it will include all that is wrought in the soul by what is frequently termed "natural conscience," but more properly "preventing grace"; —all the drawings of the Father; the desires after God, which, if we yield to them, increase more and more; —all that light wherewith the Son of God "enlighteneth every one that cometh into the world."[48]

Though both Calvin and Wesley acknowledge that this impulse is often resisted or distorted, they insist that all people are moved in one way or another to worship God or the gods. Religion is natural to them, and in this impulse God is also present.

---

[46]Saint Augustine, *Confessions*, trans. and ed. Henry Chadwick (New York: Oxford University Press, 1991).

[47]John Calvin, *Institutes of the Christian Religion*, trans. Ford Lewis Battles, ed. John T. McNeil (Philadelphia: Westminster, 1960), I.3.i.

[48]John Wesley, "The Sermons of John Wesley—Sermon 43": "The Scripture Way of Salvation," *Wesley Center Online*, III.2, accessed March 3, 2016, http://wesley.nnu.edu/john-wesley/the -sermons-of-john-wesley-1872-edition/sermon-43-the-scripture-way-of-salvation/.

In a 2000 document issued by the Congregation for the Doctrine of the Faith, *Dominus Iesus* states a similar view as representative of the Catholic Church:

> God, who desires to call all peoples to himself in Christ and to communicate to them the fullness of his revelation and love, "does not fail to make himself present in many ways, not only to individuals, but also to entire peoples through their spiritual riches, of which their religions are the main and essential expression even when they contain 'gaps, insufficiencies and errors'" [John Paul II, Encyclical Letter *Redemptoris missio*, 55]. Therefore, the sacred books of other religions, which in actual fact direct and nourish the existence of their followers, receive from the mystery of Christ the elements of goodness and grace which they contain.[49]

Of course all these theological perspectives, Protestant and Catholic, agree that Scripture provides the unique witness to the salvation that Christ offers. As the Catholic statement puts it, "these books [of Scripture] firmly, faithfully and without error teach that truth which God, for the sake of our salvation, wished to see confided to the Sacred Scriptures."[50]

This last statement on Scripture embodies a further theological conviction that undergirds and motivates Christian mission. Though all people desire to know God and seek after this God, and though this quest and the wisdom it embraces are expressed in their religion and its sacred practices and writings, the "news" about Christ is not indigenous to any culture. This is to say, God is present and active by the Spirit when the gospel is being proclaimed and Scripture read, in a way that is special and unlike the general way God is otherwise present in all cultures and religions. With all the insider movements we examined, though God was the primary agent, there also were secondary agents—missionaries, Bible translators, and teachers, those who in some way gave witness to the work of Christ and made the Scriptures available.[51] Such activity has been

---

[49]Congregation for the Doctrine of the Faith as granted by John Paul II, "Declaration '*Dominus Iesus*' on the Unicity and Salvific Universality of Jesus Christ and the Church," June 16, 2000, I.8, www .vatican.va/roman_curia/congregations/cfaith/documents/rc_con_cfaith_doc_20000806 _dominus-iesus_en.html.

[50]Ibid., II.11.

[51]While we have focused largely on insiders, we should not overlook the role of "alongsiders" in helping such movements to flourish. See the excellent chapter by John Travis and Anna Travis, "Roles of 'Alongsiders' in Insider Movements: Contemporary Examples and Biblical Reflections," in Talman and Travis, *Understanding Insider Movements*, 455-66.

central to the development of Christianity in all its many forms and gives evidence of discontinuity.

So Christians naturally ask: Despite these fundamental differences among religious traditions—or even because of them—don't Christians believe that the claims of Christianity are unique? Don't we believe that God in Christ was bringing about an actual new creation and that this project has deeply informed the development of Christianity? Simply put, despite the historically formed differences and leaving aside the question of whether Christ intended to found a new religion, is there not a basic discontinuity between Christianity and other religions?

Clearly we can say God's presence in the gospel, the news of God's re-creative and redemptive work in Christ, affirms, fulfills, challenges, and often overturns every religious situation that it encounters, but this is often true of Christianity itself. The reality is that we cannot simply conflate the work of God in Christ with Christianity. David Bosch in his discussion of Christianity and the religions notes that he finds the usual typology of religions and their relation to Christianity (e.g., exclusive, inclusive, fulfillment, relativism) unhelpful—they are too neat. Rather he thinks there are multiple and overlapping ways in which this encounter unfolds, and it demands a spiritual discernment—a meeting of hearts, not minds.[52] These various confrontations will include affirming the wisdom of the traditions here, a resistance to the errors there, and, not infrequently, an encounter with spiritual powers that actively oppose the presence of God.[53] In this more comprehensive sense we must insist on discontinuity between the gospel and religion.

---

[52]David J. Bosch, *Transforming Mission: Paradigm Shifts in Mission Theology* (Maryknoll, NY: Orbis Books, 1991), 483-84. He borrows here Max Stackhouse's encouragement to relate to other religions via *poesis* rather than *theoria*. See Max Stackhouse, *Apologia: Contextualization, Globalization and Mission in Theological Education* (Grand Rapids: Eerdmans, 1988).

[53]The presence of demonic activity in religions deserves much more attention than I am able to give it here. But it should be clear from my account of religion that, while demonic activity is present in many religious traditions (including some forms of Christianity), one would be deeply mistaken to identify non-Christian religions as inherently demonic. See on this the helpful article by Anna Travis, "In the World but Not of It: Insider Movements and Freedom from the Demonic," in Talman and Travis, *Understanding Insider Movements*, 521-36. And, for a comprehensive survey of the problems and possible responses, see Paul G. Hiebert, R. Daniel Shaw, and Tite Tiénou, *Understanding Folk Religion: A Christian Response to Popular Beliefs and Practices* (Grand Rapids: Baker Academic, 1999).

But the emphasis on "discontinuity" carries with it particular dangers that need to be recognized. Early in the last century Karl Barth famously argued that God appears to be fundamentally opposed to all human religion, even or especially "our" Christian religion. Barth's landmark commentary on *The Epistle to the Romans* presented an emphatic picture of God's grace seizing us from God's side, and not from our human side. He insisted that

> though religion and law appear to concern that relationship between men and God with which grace is also concerned, yet in fact they do not do so. . . . They stand on this [that is, the human] side of the abyss. . . . There is no stepping across the frontier by gradual advance or by laborious ascent, or by any human development whatsoever.[54]

Religion represents, he believed, this attempt of "gradual advance"; religion is therefore "the working capital of sin; its fulcrum," because it embodies the always futile, human attempt to satisfy God.[55] While Barth's critique of religion has often been seen as severe and overstated, it made a great deal of sense in the light of the liberal interpretation of Christianity of his theological teachers. And it has had a long afterlife in subsequent discussions of missions.

Barth's formulation warns us of the danger of privileging not only *some* religious practice as proof of our faith but even *our* particular Christian practices. Recall how Christ was especially critical of the leaven of the Pharisees (who, we might say, represented the Jewish evangelicals of their day) even as he seemed somewhat tolerant of those (e.g., Samaritans) the Pharisees considered outsiders. This suggests that Christ came, in part, not so much to do away with religion but to transform it from within.[56] In every case the gospel, the good news of what God was doing in Christ and in the giving of the Holy Spirit, sheds light on, enhances, and frequently corrects or confounds the wisdom that is found in human culture and in the religions of those cultures. Moreover, this gospel impulse needs constantly to be renewing even Christianity itself: as the Reformed tradition of Christianity puts this, the church is always being reformed by the Word of God (*ecclesia semper reformanda est*).

---

[54]Karl Barth, *The Epistle to the Romans*, trans. Edwyn C. Hoskyns (New York: Oxford University Press, 1922 [1919]), 240.

[55]Ibid., 248. And see Matthew Myer Boulton, *God Against Religion: Rethinking Christian Theology Through Worship* (Grand Rapids: Eerdmans, 2008), 193, 194.

[56]The notion of "transforming from within" is Boulton's interpretation of Barth's program (p. xvii).

After all, calling someone a Christian tells us little about the spiritual state of that person; it may mean a great deal or nothing at all. As we learned from chapter three, God alone is the Savior; religion in and of itself, even Christianity, does not save us.

BUT WHAT ROLE DOES SCRIPTURE PLAY?

Followers of Christ believe that there is a permanent connection between the good news that Christ brought and the Scripture. Indeed, Christians share a deep-seated conviction that God was in critical ways involved by the Spirit in the formation, collection, and preservation of these books. Nothing I say should be understood to undermine the authority of Scripture. But let me make two comments on the role that Scripture plays. First, from our discussion of biblical attitudes toward religion in the last chapter, we saw from Scripture itself that God was not interested in promoting religion in and of itself. Rather, God was working out a program of renewal and restoration that came to focus on Christ's death and resurrection and that anticipates Christ's return at the end of history. This narrative came to play a decisive role not only in the development of Christianity, which we explore momentarily, but in attitudes and responses to other religious traditions. The relationship between the gospel events and Judaism was of course the first challenge to be worked out, but there were others: for example, how does faith in Christ relate to honoring the emperor? And as we saw in chapter three, and will see again presently, answers to these challenges were not easily found. But, second, we need to remember that though Scripture is a primary witness to God's presence and work, it is never read in isolation from other factors. These include not only cultural factors but, for many people, religious traditions as well. As Kang-San Tan argues in his recent PhD dissertation, Scripture does not function as a valid criterion for evaluating other religions if their texts and teachings are not also consulted. If this does not happen, can the message of Scripture be truly comprehended?[57]

A further problem involves reading our "Christian" experience back into the New Testament. Modern readers of the New Testament are apt to see in the primitive gatherings of believers incipient worship experiences similar to

[57]Kang-San Tan, "An Examination of Dual Religious Belonging Theology: Contributions to Evangelical Missiology" (PhD diss., University of Aberdeen, 2014), 184-86.

those they know. That is, they read the New Testament through the lens of their experience as though this represents the essence of New Testament worship. But this could not have been true. Rather, faith in Christ and appropriation of the new creation he inaugurated had to take on the specific forms and rituals that were expressive of a first-century cultural identity and of the wisdom embedded in that culture. This was all that was available to them. This fact was made clear in the Scriptures themselves, especially in the rather enigmatic instructions of Acts 15, which few people would recognize today as identifiably "Christian."

Now Christians are likely to argue that Scriptures imply that certain ritual practices, such as baptism and Eucharist (or Communion), are normative for all acceptable worship. Some take dependence on the New Testament even further and insist on what is called the "regulative principle of worship," which holds that only those things specifically commanded in Scripture should be allowed in Christian worship. These divinely stipulated practices may be important, but they do not in themselves constitute a religious tradition (they were not even mentioned in the settlement of Acts 15), and they have been appropriated in widely different ways throughout the history of Western Christianity. So here is my question: Why do these elements need to be arranged in the same way that our Western post-Enlightenment heritage has decreed? If other religious patterns are formed in vastly different cultural and historical contexts, why must our particular formulation of religion be privileged? If religious practices reflect cultural differences and geographical particularities, is it not possible that other arrangements of these elements, developed in other settings, might also facilitate a true worship of God?

Earlier we discussed Jehu Hanciles's argument that the missionary movement stemming from the Protestant Reformation did nothing to dismantle the structure of Christendom. By this he means the assumption of a single model of the Christian faith that is tied invariably to Western political systems and culture. As we have seen, these colonialist assumptions have come in for heavy criticism in the last century. As Hanciles put it, by stimulating a wide variety of indigenous movements, "the message proved to be the undoing of the messenger."[58] While few missionaries harbor any illusion of

---

[58]Jehu J. Hanciles, *Beyond Christendom: Globalization, African Migration and the Transformation of the West* (Maryknoll, NY: Orbis Books, 2008), 105.

rebuilding a Christian empire, there is an important residue of this heritage; for many there is still a belief in a single normative expression of the Christian gospel. Here Hanciles's discussion is relevant. He writes:

> If the Christendom notion of one normative expression of the faith belongs to a passing era, perhaps no concept is more definitive of the new epoch than *diversity of forms and expressions*.[59]

At this point many worry that combining elements of religious traditions with the gospel can easily result in a dangerous syncretism—literally, the combining of elements of different religions. The problem of syncretism will be addressed further in the conclusion, but let me make these initial comments here. First, as we have seen from our exploration of New Testament materials and their First Testament context, what exactly was required of the first Christians was always a matter of considerable debate and uncertainty, and inevitably involved making use of the cultural materials they knew. This is understandable. It would take time and much spiritual discernment to work out what Christ's coming would mean—whether it involved only a change of direction or something more substantial. And already in the New Testament there were different ways in which faith in Christ developed expression, whether in its Jewish or its Greco-Roman context. This involved already a kind of syncretism or, better, a new synthesis. As we saw in our case studies, what to outsiders might look like an inappropriate mixture can seem to insider believers a natural response to the gospel in their setting. Kang-San Tan, as a Christian from a Buddhist background, has given much thought to this problem. He argues that if believers are to retain aspects of their previous identity, then "a certain form of double belonging is inevitable."[60] He goes on to distinguish between the danger of external identification with two religious communities and the possibility, even the necessity for those from these religious backgrounds, of maintaining an inward multireligious identity. The latter can reflect an appropriate new synthesis; the former is difficult or impossible and can be syncretistic. In fact, I will argue later that Christianity itself necessarily exhibits an integration that reflects its historical

---

[59]Ibid., 111, emphasis original.
[60]Kang-San Tan, "Can Christians Belong to More than One Religious Tradition?," *Evangelical Review of Theology* 34, no. 3 (2010): 260-61.

DOES THIS ALLOW FOR FURTHER SYNCRETISM?

and cultural situation. At this stage we might put matters this way: *Every Christian religious expression represents some combination of indigenous values and religious practices (whether one stands or sits, how one prays or offers gifts, etc.) and the impact of the Christian gospel (the work of Christ as described in Scripture) on this.*

Accordingly, as I will stress in the conclusion, I am struck by the fact that we are quick to label syncretism in others' practices but slow to recognize it in our own history. Indeed, we are mostly blind to the ways our own theology and worship practices are subtly influenced by cultural values and habits that are anything but biblical. Consider, for instance, the way racist attitudes have dogged the development of Christian worship in America.

Some will ask, no matter what form the response to Christ takes, will this not have some necessary connection if not to institutional Christianity then to what the New Testament describes as the body of Christ? Is there not also here a permanent and indelible connection? Catholics and Protestants may differ on how they define this connection, but if part of Christ's work was to call out those who would be bearers of a new humanity, some connection must be affirmed between his work and this special community. Such a community will surely display ecclesial characteristics, as Darren Duerksen put it in the last chapter. The concluding chapter will explore this question in more detail, but here I want to return one more time to the early church to see what lessons its emergent character might provide.

HOW DID THE CHRISTIAN RELIGION EMERGE?

We saw in an earlier chapter that the formation of the early Christian community (or communities) was a dynamic and contested process. But it was also a contingent, rather than a necessary, process. How Judaism, as a religion, would be impacted by the Christian gospel was a matter that was not settled easily, or soon. Interestingly, though earlier scholars felt that Christians had mostly left the synagogue toward the end of the first century after the fall of Jerusalem and the destruction of the temple (in 70 CE), now it seems clear that many disciples of Christ remained in the synagogues well into the fourth century and even beyond. A growing number of recent studies have shown how the development of Christianity over the first several centuries took place firmly within the social worlds of early Judaism (or Judaisms). Indeed, in many respects Christianity and Judaism might be seen as siblings engaging in an ongoing debate about their own future within Judaism.[61]

Evangelicals have been an active part of this conversation. Norwegian scholar Oskar Skarsaune has explored thoroughly the Jewish influences on early Christianity and notes the continuing sympathy and friendliness among the grassroots of Jews and Christians well into the fourth and even fifth century, though he acknowledges that this was probably not a majority position in either group.[62] He argues that this had mainly to do with the fact that many Christian converts were God-fearing Gentiles who visited the synagogues, and even participated in Jewish celebrations. Conversion to Christianity did not efface these Jewish sympathies, nor did it make them anti-Semitic.[63]

In a recent book, *The Jewish Gospels*, the distinguished Talmudic scholar Daniel Boyarin has elaborated on this family resemblance. Much of the central teaching of the Gospels, Boyarin argues, is not so much a departure from Jewish teaching as a specific application of this to the person of Jesus. In fact, much of Jesus' own teaching is not the innovation that it is often thought to be but a return to some of the most ancient parts of the Jewish tradition.[64] Boyarin shows the idea of a Messiah-Christ, first glimpsed in the book of Daniel, and called the Son of Man in the Gospels, was an integral part of the Jewish tradition, even in some cases understood as a second God—the appearance of a preexisting divine figure in human form. Boyarin argues that even the idea of a suffering Messiah was understood by some rabbis as a reasonable interpretation of many First Testament passages. An expanded understanding of Judaism, then, allows "for the inclusion of the earliest Gospel literature within its purview, thus making the earliest and in some ways most

---

[61]Cf. Daniel Boyarin's statement that "like many twins Judaism and Christianity never quite formed separate identities." Boyarin, *Dying for God: Martyrdom and the Making of Christianity and Judaism* (Stanford, CA: Sanford University Press, 1999), 5. For a description of this debate and the scholarly resources that are available, see Jeffrey S. Siker, "Jewish/Christian Relations at 25: Retrospect & Prospect," *Ancient Jew Review*, December 10, 2014, www.ancientjewreview.com/articles/2014/12/9/jewishchristian-relations-at-25-retrospect-prospect.

[62]Oskar Skarsaune, *In the Shadow of the Temple: Jewish Influences on Early Christianity* (Downers Grove, IL: InterVarsity Press, 2002), 442.

[63]Ibid., 440-41. See also the more complete exploration of this relationship in Oskar Skarsaune and Reidar Hvalvik, eds., *Jewish Believers in Jesus: The Early Centuries* (Peabody, MA: Hendrickson, 2007), which sought to present a fully developed history of Jewish believers in Jesus.

[64]Daniel Boyarin, *The Jewish Gospels: The Story of the Jewish Christ* (New York: New Press, 2012), 48-51.

foundational texts of Christianity—Jewish."[65] This allows one to think of Christianity as one of the paths that Judaism took, Boyarin thinks, rather than seeing it as a new invention.[66]

The possibilities inherent in this expanded vision, however, were cut off by both Christian and Jewish authorities. Boyarin notes how Jerome, the translator of the Latin Vulgate and one of the four Doctors of the Church (d. 420), was agitated by believers who had stayed in the synagogue. Boyarin writes: "If, thunders Jerome, you believe in the Nicene Creed, get out of the synagogue, and you will be a Christian. If you stay in the synagogue and drop your belief in Christian doctrine, then the Pharisees will agree to call you a Jew." Boyarin quips: "Fill in the boxes correctly on the checklist, or you are neither a Christian nor a Jew."[67] Likewise, John Chrysostom, the famous preacher and theologian in Constantinople at the end of the fourth century, lashed out at Christian believers who kept the Jewish feasts and frequented the synagogue. In his first homily, *Against the Jews*, he complains: "There are many in our ranks who say they think as we do. Yet some of these are going to watch the festivals and others will join the Jews in keeping their feasts and observing their fasts. I wish to drive this perverse custom from the Church right now."[68] Jerome and Chrysostom's outrage gives evidence that the debate over the precise relationship between these faiths continued at least through the fall of the Roman Empire and that this uncertainty deeply troubled Christian leaders. Though Christians did eventually leave the synagogue, some Jewish believers in Christ today question whether that is what God intended for Jewish people. These believers call themselves messianic Jews, and they might rightfully be considered heirs of the original insider movement in the New Testament![69]

What becomes clear in reflecting on this history is the resistance that religious leaders typically exhibit toward emerging religious forms. The tendency of institutional structures is biased on behalf of past experience. Paul DeNeui, in his study of insider movements in Buddhism, notes that pressure on these

[65]Ibid., 22-23.
[66]Ibid., 133-34.
[67]Ibid., 15-20.
[68]John Chrysostom, *Against the Jews* 1.5, accessed January 8, 2015, www.tertullian.org/fathers/chrysostom_adversus_judaeos_01_homily1.htm.
[69]Interestingly, Boyarin admits that, whether or not one accepts their theology, messianic Jews "have a very strong textual base for the view that the suffering Messiah is based in deeply rooted Jewish texts." Boyarin, *Jewish Gospels*, 133.

groups is always toward more traditional institutional forms.[70] But the New Testament seems to portray a new way of thinking about religion that is oriented toward God's future—focused not on the God of our fathers but on the emerging faith of sons and daughters. This seems to be characteristic of Paul's attitude toward "church." But as Tomáš Halík points out, the early history of the church paints a different picture.

> The church quickly withdrew into a new particularism of its own; the notion of a "new Israel" did not engender the courage to be constantly *people on the way*, boldly crossing all borders. Instead, we tended to become a "second Israel," another particular community *alongside* Israel, rather than a truly *new* Israel.[71]

Whatever one thinks about this, the extended struggle over this question—over several centuries—suggests that the relation of the gospel to other religious traditions may be more complex, and the solutions less simple, than we have made them out to be. In an important sense, as Darren Duerksen has argued, the Christian struggle to understand its relationship to the synagogue was an *emergent movement* that represented a gradual and dynamic situation of ecclesial change and development, one that stretched over a long period of time.[72]

But here I want to return to the notion of the hermeneutical spaces provided by these various encounters. Of course these spaces are often fraught, and they frequently issue in tensions of various kinds, even violence. But what if we were to think about situations like these as opportunities and not simply as problems? What if we thought of these as free spaces, not only for indigenous impulses but also for the work of the liberating Spirit? These ancient encounters (like similar ones today) offered places in which a new integration could be worked out between the gospel and the reigning perceptions and linguistic and cultural categories. And, initially at least, this process necessarily expressed values embedded in the people's original identity. People of course can change, but only when change is perceived as beneficial in their terms.

---

[70]Paul H. DeNeui, "A Typology of Approaches to Thai Folk Buddhists," in *Appropriate Christianity*, ed. Charles Kraft (Pasadena, CA: William Carey Library, 2005), 428.

[71]Tomáš Halík, *Patience with God: The Story of Zacchaeus Continuing in Us*, trans. Gerald Turner (New York: Doubleday, 2009), loc. 814, emphasis original.

[72]Darren Todd Duerksen, *Ecclesial Identities in a Multi-Faith Context: Jesus Truth-Gatherings (Yeshu Satsangs) Among Hindus and Sikhs in Northwest India* (Eugene, OR: Pickwick, 2015), chap. 11. Duerksen argues this emergent character resembles the process described in the Book of Acts.

As Daniel Shaw notes in a recent discussion of contextualization, the process is one in which people seek a new cognitive balance, or, perhaps we can say, a new "sense of things," in which old things become new, even as the new brings treasures out of the old. Note that the focus is on new forms of relationship rather than simply changing beliefs or religions.[73] And the process we have argued is a hermeneutical one; that is, people needed the space and the Spirit of God needed the freedom to work out the implications of the new information about the work of Christ within the context they knew.

While much has changed, these experiences from the New Testament can shed light on the global situation today. While there was much that remained to be worked out, certain things were clear already in the New Testament: on the one hand, specific religious practices in themselves were neither constitutive nor necessary for the reception of the salvation that Christ brought; this was to be received by warmhearted faith in Christ, as the apostles never tired of reiterating. On the other hand, the practice of religion was not optional for these new believers; their faith in Christ had to be embodied in the forms and patterns available at the time, even if these were eventually to be transformed. There is no reason to doubt that these two conditions apply today as well.

THE MISSION OF MISSIONS

Before closing this chapter I want to return briefly to the fundamental question this discussion raises. How might we define missions today in such a way that leaves room for the new forms of faith that we are exploring? While we cannot deal with this question in any detail here, it must be faced. It is an important question for many reasons, not least because the mission of the church has too often been framed in terms that explicitly disallow innovative forms of Christian community. This happens, for example, when the basic call to "make disciples of all nations" (or peoples) of Matthew 28 is read as closely advocating evangelism and church planting; where the church is understood in Western (and narrowly evangelical) categories; or when evangelism is equated with a change from one religion to another. A broader understanding of *church*,

---

[73]Cf. R. Daniel Shaw's statement: "How much energy people are willing to expend on processing information is largely a product of the perceived benefit." Shaw, "Beyond Contextualization: Toward a Twenty-first-Century Model for Enabling Mission," *International Bulletin of Missionary Research* 34, no. 4 (2010): 210-11.

something I will explore in the concluding chapter, is part of the answer. But here let me recall the argument of the earlier chapter on God's proper work of renewal and transformation—both of culture and of communities within those cultures. That is, the goal of God's work is not a perfect religion, nor merely a functioning church, but a new heaven and earth where righteousness reigns. And the Spirit of renewal is busy in every place, seeking those who will be a part of this new creation, who will together grow into the likeness of Jesus Christ. It is this larger goal that finally motivates our evangelical mission.

Making disciples of all nations, while it may well include forms of church familiar to missionaries, surely must be understood in a more inclusive way. While this book is not intended to describe what shape this might take, there are pointers in the literature to new forms of mission, beginning with David Bosch's magisterial work. Bosch notes that Jesus' ministry focused on the kingdom in which he "launches an all-out attack on evil in all its manifestations."[74] As we noted above, Bosch is convinced Jesus' intention did not include forming a new religion but calling a people to a new level of responsibility toward one another and the created order. Toward the end of his book Bosch notes that Christians' encounters with believers of other faiths should display a dialogical character. We should expect to meet God in these encounters, because, Bosch argues, in Christ God has already removed the barriers.[75]

Another recent discussion may be offered as an example. Terry Muck and Frances Adeney have proposed that mission be rethought in terms of the metaphor of gift.[76] Mission is about giving and receiving, they argue, fundamentally expressing God's receiving of human form and giving grace and eternal life in return. "What we have to offer to everyone, everywhere, is God's gift of grace."[77] Working from this metaphor allows them to begin by analyzing the central role gift giving plays in all cultures, and the way God's gift can then be understood in terms both of an acceptance of cultural practices and the subsequent reordering of those practices—as they put it, adopting a "yes . . . but" attitude. Such exchange fits well with the mutual learning that we

---

[74]Bosch, *Transforming Mission*, 32-33.

[75]Ibid., 483-84. Bosch insists, however, that one should not reduce Christian mission to dialogue because religions are often incompatible; they face, he says, different directions.

[76]Terry C. Muck and Frances S. Adeney, *Christianity Encountering World Religions: The Practice of Mission in the Twenty-First Century* (Grand Rapids: Baker Academic, 2009), 320-21.

[77]Ibid., 351.

are seeking to promote in this book. Significantly, they also show how such a rethinking can encourage a stronger Christian voice in current interreligious encounters—a voice that affirms and expresses generosity and gratitude, which is also the fundamental response required by this giving God.

CHAPTER SIX

CONCLUSION

Is God Doing Something New?

O nce, while interviewing Muslims in Los Angeles, I had arranged an interview at a mosque near my home in Altadena, California. When I arrived, I found that the man I was to interview had prepared a poster, complete with Scripture references from the Gospels arranged in the Five Pillars of Islam to demonstrate to me that Jesus was in fact a Muslim. He showed that Jesus confessed God, prayed five times a day, gave alms, and so on. I suppose I should have insisted that he had not properly understood what he read, but I felt glad that he was considering Jesus, even if it was on his own terms.[1] For what I have sought to demonstrate throughout this book is that our own terms, at the beginning, provide the only way any of us encounter Jesus. The work of transforming us into Christ's image is an act of the Spirit working in and through the experiences and patterns of our lives. Though it will not be complete until we stand perfected in God's presence, it always begins with the impressions of faith and religious experiences that we bring with us.

That work of transforming people into Christ's image is a central aspect of the larger work of God that we call the kingdom or the reign of God. I contend that all the groups we consider—what we call insider and emergent movements—must be seen and evaluated not initially in the light of the Christian church but in terms of this larger redemptive rule of God in the world. I say

---

[1]As we saw in J. Dudley Woodberry's article, cited previously, I might even have argued that in fact Muhammad developed these Five Pillars under the influence of Judaism and Christianity; cf. Woodberry, "Contextualization Among Muslims: Reusing Common Pillars," in *Understanding Insider Movements: Disciples of Jesus Within Diverse Religious Communities*, ed. Harley Talman and John Jay Travis (Pasadena, CA: William Carey Library, 2015), 407-35.

"initially" because eventually we will have to ask how these should relate to the worldwide body of Christ we call the church—and this is something we will attempt to answer in this concluding chapter. To begin with, we need to be clear about our priorities. What is of supreme value to God, what we called in the second chapter the proper work of God, is the renewing of creation in Jesus Christ by the power of the Spirit so that it comes to fully reflect God's glory. The church of course is meant to play a critical role in this project, but we need to recall that it is the kingdom that creates the church, not the other way around.[2] Moreover, God's purposes and renewing activity extend beyond the confines of the church. God seeks nothing less than a new creation when

> the earth will be full of the knowledge of the LORD
> as the waters cover the sea. (Is 11:9)

It is for this reason I have insisted on holding together "insider" and "emergent" movements, for these together in their many forms evince the larger work of God, wherein the Spirit is drawing all things together in Christ. Insider movements as defined by Scott Moreau, we recall, are "movements to obedient faith in Christ that remain integrated with or *inside* their natural community."[3] Moreau goes on to note two distinct elements contained in such movements: (1) As the gospel takes root in these preexisting communities, Moreau claims, it becomes an expression of "church" in that place. Believers are not extracted from this setting to become members of the church, and (2) this allows believers to retain their identity as members of their original communities while living under the lordship of Christ.[4] This is helpful in its insistence that insofar as these groups exhibit ecclesial identities, they are formed in ways consistent with their natural community. But we need to ask: How do we understand the "church" being formed in these communities? And how might this impact our understanding of mission?

Moreau describes a spectrum of such movements, ranging from traditional Christian churches functioning without adaptation within other

---

[2]This was a central part of the argument George Eldon Ladd made a generation ago in his hugely influential book, *Jesus and the Kingdom: The Eschatology of Biblical Realism* (New York: Harper & Row, 1964).

[3]A. Scott Moreau, *Contextualization in World Missions: Mapping and Assessing Evangelical Models* (Grand Rapids: Kregel, 2012), 161, emphasis original.

[4]Ibid., 161-66.

religious settings, what are called C1 movements, to those that adapt in various ways to their settings, the most hidden group being C6, those who must practice their faith in secret.[5] Helpful as such typologies are, there is an implicit danger that such categorization is part of an (outsider) Christian attempt to discern where we need to "draw the line." In other words, it all too easily reflects a Western metanarrative that is used to judging what is appropriate contextualization and what is clearly "subchristian." I believe the problem with all such approaches is that they fail to understand the dynamic and interactive character of all such groups on the one hand and the core theological nature of the church within the larger program of God on the other. In this concluding chapter I will seek to explain and defend these claims before moving, too briefly, to a final discussion of the theological nature of the church.

EMERGENT MOVEMENTS

Coming to understand the claims of Christ and responding to these in appropriate ways is often an extended process, whether for the individual or the community. For various historical and theological reasons, the dominant model of conversion that missions have traditionally embraced involves a clean break with the past—what Willie Jennings has described as creation ex nihilo.[6] A primary source for this view is the model of Christianity stemming from the Reformation, described in the first chapter. By this model, faith in Christ, shorn of all ritual and cultural elements, could be fitted into any cultural situation (by the process later called contextualization). But a subsequent and not unrelated source for this model was an assumption of the superiority of Western culture that missionaries (often unconsciously) embraced, prompting an approach that sought to extract converts from their culture and "develop" them in ways consistent with Western culture. Happily, missionaries are increasingly alert to these dangers and mostly recognize the responsibility of local believers to find appropriate ways to hear and obey Scripture and follow Christ. Most would agree with Scott Sunquist's

---

[5]Ibid. Moreau's source for the C-spectrum is John Travis, "The C1 to C6 Spectrum," *Evangelical Missions Quarterly* 34, no. 4 (1998): 407-8.

[6]Willie James Jennings, *The Christian Imagination: Theology and the Origins of Race* (New Haven, CT: Yale University Press, 2010), 81-82.

assessment that "appropriate cultural expressions usually come out of the local community of believers."[7]

Another source for this assumption that conversion is a break from one's past is the dominant understanding of conversion among evangelicals. A common tenet of evangelical faith is the call to be "born again." Ostensibly this view is drawn from the narrative of Jesus with Nicodemus in John 3, where Jesus tells Nicodemus, "No one can see the kingdom of God without being born from above" (Jn 3:3). But in reality the new-birth theology owes as much or more to its American setting, where people are anxious for the chance to start afresh with a clean slate and live a new life.[8] Of course we should not discount the possibility or the reality of radical conversions, from the time of the apostle Paul to the present. And in many places of the world, turning to Christ does—indeed must—involve a clean break with the past, especially when this past involves actual spiritual bondage.[9] But, even in such cases, it is often a mistake to expect such changes to happen quickly or easily. Just as the early Christians struggled over their relation to Judaism, so many today will anguish over the push and pull of their previous relationships. It has become increasingly clear that the New Testament itself does not endorse the necessity of sudden dramatic conversions but highlights the need to grow into understanding and obedience over time.[10]

Identifying these changes as a process of growth recognizes that all the movements we are concerned with are in one way or another "emergent"; that is, they exist in a dynamic environment under the influence of multiple factors. Christian Smith describes this: "Emergence refers to the process of constituting a new entity with its own particular characteristics . . . through the interactive combination of other different entities that are necessary to create the new entity."[11] This allows something new to emerge that was not present before, even if it carries forward important inherited characteristics.

---

[7]Scott W. Sunquist, *Understanding Christian Mission: Participation in Suffering and Glory* (Grand Rapids: Baker Academic, 2013), 256.

[8]For a more complete expression of this theme see William A. Dyrness, *How Does America Hear the Gospel?* (Grand Rapids: Eerdmans, 1989), chap. 4.

[9]Sunquist makes this point in *Understanding Christian Mission*, 257. He notes that frequently the new believers themselves decide to reject previous practices, causing many to experience conversion as a "disenculturation."

[10]See, for example, Richard V. Peace's argument that a process of conversion is the fundamental teaching of the Gospels: *Conversion in the New Testament: Paul and the Twelve* (Grand Rapids: Eerdmans, 1999).

[11]Christian Smith, *To Flourish or Destruct: A Personalist Theory of Human Goods, Motivations, Failure, and Evil* (Chicago: University of Chicago Press, 2015), 36.

At this point it might be helpful to consider an important parallel conversation that we have hinted at throughout the book: what is called the emergent church movement in America and Europe. There are important differences between emergent and insider movements of course, but the parallels are significant in at least two respects. First, adherents of emergent movements in many cases display a deep dissatisfaction with current forms of the Christian church and the desire to distance themselves from these. Second, these groups, responding to various cultural influences, which they seek constructively to embrace, mirror the often inchoate and flexible nature of processes observed in insider movements—specifically their "emergent" character.

Eddie Gibbs and Ryan Bolger, in their important study of emergent churches, interviewed more than fifty leaders from groups throughout Europe and North America. These leaders frequently expressed the need to distance themselves from the institutional church, which was perceived to be out of touch or insensitive to the spiritual needs of people.[12] The authors became accustomed to hearing stories about the desire to dismantle inherited church practices that were no longer responsive to cultural longings. Gibbs and Bolger conclude that typical church responses to cultural changes are mostly surface changes—adding a youth service here, attending to generational differences there. Taking their cue from what they believe God is doing in the kingdom, these emergent groups seek a more radical transformation. Gibbs and Bolger summarize their findings: "Emergent churches utilize the kingdom as a tool to deconstruct all aspects of life, including virtually all church practices."[13]

What practices do they see as reflecting the kingdom work of God? Just as Darren Duerksen found in his research in North India, Gibbs and Bolger came across evidence of a rather consistent ecclesial program that emerged in the course of their interviews. They found that these groups strongly identify with Jesus and see in him an "invitation to participate with God in the redemption of the world."[14] The groups seek to embody a visible communal life—a visible righteousness that resembles a family rather than a congregation. There is a strong determination to reach out and welcome the stranger—not so much to have a social program, but to *be* a social program, to live a "socially engaged

---

[12]Eddie Gibbs and Ryan K. Bolger, *Emerging Churches: Creating Christian Community in Postmodern Cultures* (Grand Rapids: Baker Academic, 2005), 46, 94.

[13]Ibid., 96.

[14]Ibid., 64.

way of life." Finally, these groups insist that they must stay engaged with the wider culture and respond to its needs.[15] Indeed, their practices reflect a consistent determination to respond to postmodern culture *for the sake* of their witness to Christ. A group in Brussels is active in community projects funded by the city; that is their outreach. Another in Seattle engages with the local Fremont Arts Council and works with them on the winter solstice events, proposing there a prayerful Ignatian *examen* of light.[16]

These efforts are emergent, and thus necessarily vulnerable and fragile; they are in the process of becoming. So in a sense the emerging church is as much a goal as it is a reality. As these authors note, this is not only true of emergent church experiments; it is also true of the church in any form: "The church universal is an emerging church, for as the body of Christ here on earth, it awaits with eager anticipation the return of its Lord. As such, it is a church always in the process of becoming."[17]

It is possible to see these groups as contemporary forms of the perennial impetus to renew the structures of the church that have appeared throughout church history, from the medieval mendicants, through the Reformation and revivals, and up to the Pentecostal and charismatic movements of the last century. In this respect they are evidence of the continuing presence of the Spirit of God, who continues to form the body of Christ into maturity in Christ. Though there are many differences, emergent and insider movements both reflect God's wider purposes in the world and take their cue not primarily from the Christian tradition but from their direct encounter with Christ in their situation and from their fresh reading of the Scripture. Among the most significant differences is the fact that these emergent groups still work within the general framework of historical Christianity, and therefore are easy for us to appreciate. But is it possible for us to believe that God is at work beyond the confines of Christianity? Is there some sense that the universal body of Christ, and not simply the work of the kingdom, can be present at least in some inchoate form within other religions?

---

[15]Ibid., 142, 233.

[16]See Blayne Waltrip, "European Longings for the Kingdom: Pentecostal Reflections on Living Out the Kingdom of God Missionally and Incarnationally in Western Europe" (PhD diss., Fuller Theological Seminary, 2011). For the Brussels community see Waltrip; for the Seattle group see Gibbs and Bolger, *Emerging Churches*, 177.

[17]Gibbs and Bolger, *Emerging Churches*, 43.

POSSIBLE ESTIMATIONS OF INSIDER MOVEMENTS

Turning specifically to the insider movements we considered in our case studies, I will examine their relationships to the larger body of Christ. But before doing that I want to review the various ways these groups have been evaluated and how Christian leaders have typically reacted to them.[18]

The first possible (and not uncommon) response to such movements is outright rejection. There are those who want missionaries, and the global church more generally, to have nothing to do with such groups, because, in their minds, these groups constitute a serious threat to the purity of the gospel message and the essence of evangelism. In the minds of these leaders, these specific theological commitments (including, for example, certain convictions about the Trinity or specific formulations of the work of Christ) are of such paramount importance that unqualified support of these movements is unthinkable. Beyond stating it, I will not belabor this option, nor offer examples, because it is not clear to me what such disapproval might mean in practice. Surely we are not meant to actively discourage those who so earnestly seek Christ and desire to follow him. And why would we want to actively remove support from those who seek to minister in such settings? Such counterproductive strategies remind me of the account of a certain missionary in Africa working with an indigenous movement. Since this movement was known to promote some strange (and perhaps unbiblical) teachings, friends asked him how he could work with these people. His response is relevant to our discussion: And what did you think mission was all about; has it not always been about working with groups who have imperfect awareness of God and seeking to bring them to maturity in Christ?

The second, and more common, response is an assumption that movements of this kind are transitional. They represent liminal spaces in which people make their way out of their past life and find a new life in Christ and, eventually, find their place in the Christian church. When I asked a friend and former schoolmate who had worked for years with Muslims in Central Asia how he evaluated those believers from a Muslim background who decided to

[18]See the conclusion reached in "Bridging the Divide," which resulted from an eponymous private colloquium on insider movements sponsored by the Lausanne continuing committee in June 2015 and held in Ghana: "Given the complexity of contexts, a diversity of approaches is to be expected" (p. 1).

remain in the mosque, his response was that in his experience such situations were mostly temporary. While they may for a time seek to maintain ties with their community and continue its practices, sooner or later, whether because of the pressures of that culture or the attraction of the Christian culture, they move to join the visible Christian groups. (And our study of Christianity's relation to Judaism reminds us that such transitions may extend over long periods of time.) There is clearly wisdom in this observation, but as with the previous option it does not provide any particular guidance as to how we are to engage with these movements. Moreover, the assumption of its transitional state implies that movement toward the traditional Christian church is the desired outcome when, as we have seen, often these believers perceive this as an outcome to be resisted at all costs. Even if this is what might eventually happen, why should we not respond like Gamaliel in Acts 5:38-39, who advised: "Let them alone; because if this plan or this undertaking is of human origin, it will fail; but if it is of God, you will not be able to overthrow them—in that case you may even be found fighting against God!"

This leads me to explore a third response that has been proposed: that we think of insider and emergent movements, in all their various forms and permutations, as places where God is at work and where something new is emerging. Those who argue along these lines see these places as hermeneutical spaces in which people attracted to Christ are working out the sense of this new life in the light of the cultural and even religious resources at hand—in much the same way that early Christians sought to determine what their new allegiance to Christ meant to their Jewish identity. The important point is that Christ had introduced a new element into the religious life of Judaism that would be the means of renewing not only Judaism but eventually the entire created order. As Dietrich Bonhoeffer notes, wherever the name of Jesus is spoken, even ignorantly or with hesitation, "it creates for itself a space to which the revilement of Jesus has no access, a region which still belongs to the power of Christ, where one must not interfere and hinder but where one must allow the name of Jesus Christ to do its work."[19] This is good advice, and it is consistent with Gamaliel's counsel in Acts. These movements represent

---

[19]Dietrich Bonhoeffer, *Ethics*, ed. Eberhard Bethge, trans. N. H. Smith (New York: MacMillan, 1955), 57. Bonhoeffer goes on to speak of the power that always accompanies the speaking of this name.

places where Christ is being named, and we should be careful to honor the ways the Spirit may be at work. Certainly this means at the very least carefully listening to those involved.

While much of the earlier literature on this phenomenon has been written by outsiders eager to judge or evaluate, recently a growing literature has sought to listen and learn from those on the ground. My purpose has been to listen carefully to these, and I have made use of those available to me in the chapter of case studies. So the relevant question is, how do these (insider) voices evaluate what is happening in these movements?

Perhaps the most helpful model emerging from such sources is something we might call "dual belonging." In various forms this notion of duality emerges in many of the most recent reflections on insider movements. In his study of Arab believers of Muslim background who have become believers, Jens Barrett has found that many of them simply refused to choose between their Muslim and their Christian identities.[20] He concludes that their Christian and Muslim identities are not "monolithic" or "mutually exclusive." Referring to Thani, one of these Arab believers, Barrett notes: "In refusing to choose a single cultural allegiance, Thani's identity cannot be located on the much debated 'C-spectrum.'"[21] Using the analogy of immigration, Barrett proposes that even if these believers have emigrated from Islam to Christianity, there is a part of them that is still deeply Muslim. Islam remains these believers' "homeland."[22] As Kang-San Tan argues, if one is to retain aspects of a previous identity—a new primary affiliation along with an older secondary one—"a certain form of double belonging is inevitable."[23] Indeed, it may be the necessary result of interfaith encounters for believers from these backgrounds, and it may result not in syncretism but a new arena of discipleship.

Another way of thinking about this is to consider that believers in this situation display a dialogical self; they have come to accept a new identity without completely giving up their previous one. In general these observers resist the

---

[20]Jens Barrett, "Refusing to Choose: Multiple Belonging Among Arab Followers of Christ," in *Longing for Community: Church, Ummah, or Somewhere in Between?*, ed. David Greenlee (Pasadena, CA: William Carey, 2013), 19-28.

[21]Ibid., 20.

[22]Ibid., 21.

[23]Kang-San Tan, "Can Christians Belong to More Than One Religious Tradition" (unpublished article, 8, used by permission).

idea that these selves are blended. In another study Barrett has noted that these liminal spaces often become "semiotic battlegrounds," where values are being assessed and a new integration is sought—allowing new meanings to emerge from this newly defined (and contested) space. He goes on to describe a process he calls "cultural frame shifting," in which different cultural frames are applied in the relevant situations and new understandings emerge. When Barrett asked another believer, Thalit, how his faith in Christ affects his identity as a Muslim, Thalit responded, "My faith [in Christ] makes me a better Muslim."[24]

Of course this all has elicited strong resistance on the part of some Christian leaders. In a recent review of David Greenlee's book (in which Barrett's studies appear), Michael Nazir-Ali warns of the danger of Christ followers (or seekers) lapsing into a dhimmi mentality—that is, someone formed by the Muslim covenant. Missionary projects, he thinks, should avoid accommodating themselves to this "*Dhimmi* framework." This assumes, he argues, that one must make a proper distinction between religion and culture.[25] But as we have stressed, for many people in this situation separating these worlds is impossible. But the deeper problem is that the dhimmi framework is the only framework these people have; their very identities rest on this, in the same way that our identities rest on the framework we bring to our faith. So to require one to escape from this, as a kind of precondition to hearing the news of Christ, is to raise an insurmountable barrier. We can expect that following out the implications of this news will lead to change, just as our reception of the gospel led to our transformation, but we ought not require that they adopt a foreign framework before they can properly hear this news or begin to work out its implications.

Meanwhile, we need to recognize that there is important theological work being done as part of the struggle of these followers of Christ. David Smilde, in his striking study of Christian conversion in Latin America, has noted how

[24]Jens Barrett, "Living a Pun: Cultural Hybridity Among Arab Followers of Christ," in Greenlee, *Longing for Community*, 33. See also pp. 35, 37.

[25]Michael Nazir-Ali, "Longing for Community: Church, Ummah, or Somewhere Between? A Review Essay," *International Bulletin of Missionary Research* 39, no. 1 (2015): 39. *Dhimmi* is a contraction of *Ahl al Dhimma*, the Arabic expression that refers to the people formed by a covenant. *Dhimmi* refers to people who possess the status conferred on "people of the (revealed) scripture" (*Ahl al-kitab*), that is, members of the Muslim community.

Christians in these settings have found imaginative ways to respond to the challenges of their contexts. These Christians, he says, express in their everyday cultural practices a "creative agency." Conversion to evangelicalism provides these believers with "a form of cultural agency through which they can gain control over aspects of their personal and social contexts."[26] Insider believers in Christ certainly demonstrate a similar creative agency that allows them to negotiate between their newfound faith in Christ and their inherited identity and practices. Smilde describes this creativity in what he terms a new "imaginative rationality." Significantly, this method seeks to preserve both cultural autonomy and personal agency; that is, it allows the preservation of inherited cultural processes while encouraging fresh personal reflection. He explains: "People [in such situations] encounter problems, create new projects to address them and then reflectively evaluate the success of these projects." They get things done by creating new concepts.[27] We could say similar things about insider believers. Working with their received notions—of the teaching of the Buddha, of Muhammad as prophet, or of popular religious practices— these believers may have eyes to see fresh dimensions of God's renewing work in Christ that outsiders cannot see.[28] More to the point, these groups may represent a critical movement of people toward recognizing and embracing this work of Christ.[29]

For our part, there may be further theological work sparked by reflection on insider movements. Western Christians may be able to see more clearly the synthesis that has resulted in their own received Christianity. We may see, for example, ways in which the whole Christian tradition has been so thoroughly influenced by the Greco-Roman legal and philosophical heritage that

---

[26]David Smilde, *Reason to Believe: Cultural Agency in Latin American Evangelicalism* (Berkeley: University of California Press, 2007), 5.

[27]Ibid., 52. Smilde goes on to develop a parallel "relational imagination," wherein relationships can either encourage or discourage movement: "People are often spurred to imagine alternatives through contact in their households with people embodying those alternatives" (p. 155).

[28]Some of the most promising explorations in this regard are to be found in the articles collected in Melba Padilla Maggay, ed., *The Gospel in Culture: Contextualization Issues Through Asian Eyes* (Manila: OMF Literature/ISACC, 2013).

[29]This can be helpfully understood in the terms of the set theory that Paul G. Hiebert proposed a generation ago. He asked what it might mean to think of the church not in terms of a bounded set—asking who's "in" and who's "out"—but as a centered set that asks whether the direction of movement is toward Christ. See Hiebert, "The Category of *Christian* in the Mission Task," in *Anthropological Reflections on Missiological Issues* (Grand Rapids: Baker Academic, 1994), 107-36, parts of which had been published as early as 1978.

it is no longer possible for us to separate what derives directly from biblical revelation and what comes from this synthesis. To take but one example, biblical anthropology has long insisted that the Christian hope involves an integrated soul and body, not simply an immortal soul existing separately from the body. Now this is clearly a biblical idea, but as we have framed this in our theology, it is also an Aristotelian idea. In fact, A. N. Williams has argued that in its detailed elaboration in Western theology during the Middle Ages, this conception owes more to Aristotle than to the Bible. But, she argues, this is not a case of pagan philosophy subverting Christianity (i.e., syncretism); rather, it is an example of philosophy having been "co-opted to underscore a deeply Christian view."[30]

The implications of this for future theological reflection should be clear. Western Christians have been the recipients, for better or worse, of influences from many directions in constructing their theology. Why should not those from widely different traditions be allowed to appropriate (and co-opt) elements from their tradition in the service of their own theological reflection? Why should they continue to be colonized by a Western synthesis of the gospel? The theological work they do appropriating their Confucian or Indic heritage is not in principle any different from that done by our forefathers and mothers in rereading Plato and Aristotle. Indeed, as Elsa Tamez has demonstrated, without biblically informed reflection on these layers, not only will missiology fail to find traction, but we will not be in a position to learn from these new angles of vision. In the end this may be the most important theological dividend of reflection on insider movements: to dare to imagine faith in Christ appearing in a wholly new idiom.

Remember, we can expect these new insights because theologically we insist with Kang-San Tan that the Spirit of God is at work in these border zones. As he says,

> At his deepest being and self, God hears the call of the Minaret, Temple chants, Buddhist prayers as human aspirations for relationship with the divine. The Christian message is that Jesus is the human face of God welcoming all true religious aspirations.[31]

---

[30]A. N. Williams, "The Theology of the *Comedy*," in *Cambridge Companion to Dante*, ed. Rachel Jacoff, 2nd ed. (Cambridge: Cambridge University Press, 2007), 210.

[31]Kang-San Tan, "Beyond Demonising Religions: A Biblical Framework for Interfaith Relations in

BUT WHERE IS THE CHURCH?

But the most difficult question remains: if we grant that God is at work calling people to become disciples of Christ, are such groups part of the Christian church? And, if so, how can this be understood? Often this question is asked as though relationship to the traditional Christian churches should be fairly straightforward and unproblematic. These new believers need to join with other Christians whatever the cost might be. Despite this frequent admonition, this is never a simple move. In a recent response to a collection of articles by young Asian theologians, Hispanic scholar Carlos Cardoza-Orlandi noted that these scholars referred to "church" frequently in a manner that seemed to hover above the complex dynamics of Asian cultures. He went on: "This generic reference to the 'church' assumes a static and triumphalistic ecclesiology—what I call a typical 'Protestant micro-Christendom.'" This construal of things, Cardoza-Orlandi argues, is a legacy of the Western missionary movement and may hamper "the potential for unique Asian ecclesiologies, grounded in the interplay between mission and what it means to be the church on Asian soil."[32] Similarly, I would argue that imposing a notion of the church on emergent movements could well obscure our ability to discover new forms of church.

Western theologians, naturally, are likely to defer to historical treatments of the church. On the one hand, these are likely to stress the theological *nature* of the church, as in the Nicene Creed, which states, "We believe in one holy catholic and apostolic Church." On the other hand, such definitions may stress the normative *functions* that define the church, as in Calvin's famous claim that "wherever we see the word of God purely preached and heard, and the sacraments administered according to Christ's institution, there, it is not to be doubted, a Church of God exists." But Calvin goes on to insist that though this church is dispersed in various places, it "agrees on the one truth of divine doctrine, and is bound by the bond of the same religion."[33] Though these approaches provide helpful starting points, they all reflect their own special cultural and theological situations. The one sought to underline the unity and holiness of the church in the face of heresies that threatened; the other focused

Asia," *Church and Society in Asia Today* 15 (December 2012): 192.

[32]Carlos Cardoza-Orlandi, "An Invitation to Theological Dialogue," in *What Young Asian Theologians Are Thinking*, ed. Leow Theng Huat (Singapore: Trinity Theological College, 2014), 132.

[33]John Calvin, *Institutes of the Christian Religion*, ed. John McNeill, trans. Ford Lewis Battles (Philadelphia: Westminster, 1960), IV.1.9.

on the recovery of the gospel truth the Reformers felt had been lost during the medieval period. As we saw, this emphasis on function was intended to replace the medieval rituals, which had been subject to abuse, with a more biblical set of practices.

But what if the vastly different settings represented by insider groups offer challenges for which these earlier episodes have not prepared us? What if the special situations described in our case studies, these hermeneutical spaces, provide unique opportunities to explore new ecclesial forms? I find it helpful in this context to recall the pivotal Roman Catholic discussion of the nature of the church presented in the papal encyclical of 2000, *Dominus Iesus*. In the section on the church in its relation to other groups that confess Christ (which include all those not in communion with the Catholic church, including Protestant groups), the document notes that the church of Christ exists fully only within the Catholic Church. Nevertheless, outside of this structure "'many elements can be found of sanctification and truth,' that is, in those churches and ecclesial communities which are not yet in full communion with the Catholic Church."[34] The document goes on to insist that finally the church and the kingdom cannot be separated any more than Christ can be separated from the kingdom, inasmuch as the church is the body of Christ on earth, even if the working of Christ and the Spirit extends outside of the visible church.

This is an important statement for many reasons, not least for its ecumenical significance. But Protestants might also suggest that a similar relationship exists between the visible church and those groups outside of it—in various insider and emergent movements, which may also exhibit "sanctification and truth." That is, they may in fact be ecclesial communities not yet in full communion. Though this may seem to support an understanding of these groups as transitional, this is not necessarily so. Certainly no Protestant I know feels their church is *necessarily* destined for full communion with the Catholic Church!

Indeed, much recent thinking of the church, influenced perhaps by the challenges offered by the emergent movement, has come to stress less the

---

[34]Congregation for the Doctrine of the Faith as granted by John Paul II, "Declaration '*Dominus Iesus*' on the Unicity and Salvific Universality of Jesus Christ and the Church," June 16, 2000, IV.16, www .vatican.va/roman_curia/congregations/cfaith/documents/rc_con_cfaith_doc_20000806_dominus -iesus_en.html. The embedded quotation is from Second Vatican Council, *Lumen Gentium*, 15.

institutional structure than the role these communities play in forming people into the likeness of Christ, that is, as places where the redemptive and renewing work of God is celebrated and progressively realized. The recent document "Bridging the Divide," resulting from a discussion of those involved in insider movements, began its statement on the church in this way: "The church as the people of God is a sign and instrument of the kingdom."[35] This is a helpful reminder that God's work of renewal extends beyond the visible church.

Many contemporary treatments of the church develop this larger theme. In one typical study, Craig Van Gelder recognizes the church's dual nature as both "God's personal presence in the world by the Spirit"—that is, a spiritual community—and as a social reality having some social structure.[36] He goes on to note that this reality is necessarily developmental as believers seek to live out this new community, demonstrating God's redemptive reign in the broader community. The church then is best seen as "a people shaped by the redemptive reign of God"; that is, the church is a means to the realization of this reign and not an end in itself.[37]

Similarly, Patrick Oden has recently argued that the church exists as a transformative agent of God's purposes in the world. A community is transformative, Oden argues, if "it engages in the development of people to better reflect the life of Christ in their lives."[38] Significantly, Oden claims such groups are embedded in their communities, not separate from them; they become an identity-forming system within larger identity-forming entities. The church in this reading is the actualization of God's re-creative purposes in a community, wherein people and communities of such people find new life in Christ by the Spirit, a life that is communal and participatory.

These statements resonate with the important discussion of the church in Bosch, *Transforming Mission*, where he argues that "the church is always and only a preliminary community, en route to its self-surrender unto the kingdom of God."[39] It is always tied to the person of Christ and oriented toward the

[35]"Bridging the Divide," 3.
[36]Craig Van Gelder, *The Essence of the Church: A Community Created by the Spirit* (Grand Rapids: Baker Books, 2000), 25.
[37]Ibid., 89; see also pp. 42-43.
[38]Patrick Oden, *The Transformative Church: New Ecclesial Models and the Theology of Jürgen Moltmann* (Minneapolis: Fortress, 2015), 5-6.
[39]David J. Bosch, *Transforming Mission: Paradigm Shifts in Mission Theology* (Maryknoll, NY: Orbis Books, 1991), 169. This is in the context of his discussion of Pauline ecclesiology.

future culmination of all things in God. It is always the beginning of the new age, not its conclusion, and it always points beyond itself.

In this sense the church is always oriented toward a future that God is bringing about. And since it is a byproduct of the resurrection of Jesus, it must always be ready to do as Paul did, "forgetting what lies behind and straining forward to what lies ahead" (Phil 3:13). Here the comments of Tomáš Halík are especially apt for our argument: "The church should constantly come out from its Christian past and have the capacity to leave much of its 'heritage' boldly behind it. This was and still is its task." We are always, Halík notes, "people on the way."[40]

These studies recall Paul's reminder in Ephesians 4:11-16 of the essential nature of the ministries of Christ: multiple gifts are for the sake of building up the members into the likeness of Christ, "until all of us come to the unity of the faith and of the knowledge of the Son of God, to maturity, to the measure of the full stature of Christ" (Eph 4:13). If we take this perspective as our starting point, we can shift our attention away from social structure and its traditional forms to the Spirit-led purposes for which these exist—that is, bringing people to maturity in Christ. We might further suggest that wherever this purpose is being realized, however imperfectly, this place constitutes an incipient ecclesial form, containing many elements of "sanctification and truth."

Clearly it is not possible for us to propose a definitive ecclesiology for insider movements. That is something that needs to be explored with the help of those within these movements.[41] At this stage we can merely highlight the emerging ecclesial elements that are visible from the available accounts, and from our outsider perspective. From an examination of our case studies we can say that these movements are characterized by four common and typical elements that often appear to contribute to emergent forms of church. First, their focus is consistently centered on devotion to Christ—in prayer, song, and biblical reflection, even if Christ is frequently put in conversation with Buddha or Muhammad. Second, we have noticed that these groups typically privilege Scripture—whether sung or taught—even if it is read and compared

[40]Tomáš Halík, *Patience with God: The Story of Zacchaeus Continuing in Us*, trans. Gerald Turner (New York: Doubleday, 2009), loc. 812. As we saw earlier, he goes on to note how often in its history the church withdrew into a "new particularism."
[41]This is to be the focus of a forthcoming book by Darren Todd Duerksen and William A. Dyrness: *Discovering the Church*.

with other sacred writings. Third, these groups all exhibit various forms of visible fellowship (what the New Testament calls *koinōnia*), even if, again, these communities are not meant to stand apart from their cultural context. Finally, these groups invariably reflect a deep desire to witness to their faith in Christ within their natural relational networks.

Sometimes less evident is conscious identification of insider movements with other parts of the body of Christ. The "Bridging the Divide" consensus document, in the section on ecclesiology, notes: "These local communities should be in communion with the wider body of Christ (local, worldwide and historical)." The document goes on to observe how these groups are "finding ways to identify themselves without using the common local term for 'church,' but are still finding ways to relate to already existing churches."[42] This process, like much else, is determined and perhaps constricted by the specific circumstances of their context, and it gives further evidence of their emergent character.

This difficulty of affiliation and identity reflects what might be the fundamental challenge faced by insider movements: how to negotiate the tension between identification with their community and the call to follow Christ in the larger project of God's kingdom purposes. A generation ago Andrew Walls famously described this dilemma as the conflict between two principles: the indigenizing and pilgrim principles.[43] On the one hand, God calls believers to be salt and light in their communities, to allow the gospel, which is at home in every culture, to be leaven that works from within the processes of their time and place. On the other hand, we are called out of this place to be citizens of a kingdom that is ahead of us, toward which we journey together as pilgrims. This latter principle is disorienting. Being faithful to Christ will surely sooner or later put us out of step with our own culture. Walls writes, "That society never existed in East or West, ancient time or modern, which could absorb the word of Christ painlessly into its system."[44] For though the gospel can transform a culture, it can also become its prisoner. Though this may perhaps be a special temptation for insider movements, their challenge is a

---

[42]"Bridging the Divide," 3.
[43]Andrew Walls, "The Gospel as the Prisoner and Liberator of Culture," *Missionalia* 10, no. 4 (1982): 93-105.
[44]Ibid., 99.

reminder that all of us must struggle with this dual identity as we seek that city which is above.

When we consider our response to this new reality, we surely must begin with gratitude for the evidences of the working of the Holy Spirit. But equally clear is our call to accompany these brothers and sisters in their journey toward the renewal of all things in Christ by the Spirit. The way ahead for many of them is filled with challenges most of us cannot imagine. Witness for us surely must be centrally one of solidarity, encouragement, and prayer.

In the congregation where I worship each week we frequently pray:

> Lord Jesus Christ, grow and sustain your church throughout the world, and empower your people to be witnesses to your life and your resurrection. Bring wisdom, courage and discernment to all those who lead, that they may faithfully pass on what has been entrusted to them.

As I pray, I think of small groups of followers of Christ in all kinds of difficult settings and emerging communities throughout the world who seek to follow Christ, and I cannot imagine that they are not included in the scope of this prayer.

BIBLIOGRAPHY

Accad, Martin. "Christian Attitudes Toward Islam and Muslims: A Kerygmatic Approach." In *Understanding Insider Movements*, edited by Harley Talman and John Jay Travis, 437-53. Pasadena, CA: William Carey Library, 2015

Acoba, E. (pseudonym), "Towards an Understanding of Inclusivity in Contextualizing into Philippine Context." In *The Gospel in Culture: Contextualization Issues Through Asian Eyes*, edited by Melba Padilla Maggay, 416-50. Manila: OMF Literature/ISACC, 2013.

Armstrong, Karen. *Muhammad: A Prophet for Our Time*. San Francisco: Harper-Collins, 2006.

———. *Fields of Blood: Religion and the History of Violence*. New York: Knopf, 2014.

Asad, Talal. *Genealogies of Religion: Discipline and Reasons of Power in Christianity and Islam*. Baltimore: Johns Hopkins University Press, 1994.

———. *Formations of the Secular: Christianity, Islam and Modernity*. Palo Alto, CA: Stanford University Press, 2003.

Augustine, Aurelius. *Confessions*. Translated and edited by Henry Chadwick. New York: Oxford University Press, 1991.

Barrett, David B. *Schism and Renewal in Africa: An Analysis of Six Thousand Religious Movements*. New York: Oxford University Press, 1968.

Barrett, Jens. "Refusing to Choose: Multiple Belonging Among Arab Followers of Christ." In *Longing for Community: Church, Ummah, or Somewhere in Between?*, edited by David Greenlee, 19-28. Pasadena, CA: William Carey, 2013.

Barth, Karl. *Epistle to the Romans*. New York: Oxford University Press, 1933.

Bartholomew, Craig G., and Ryan P. O'Dowd, *Old Testament Wisdom Literature: A Theological Introduction*. Downers Grove, IL: InterVarsity Press, 2011.

Bediako, Kwame. *Christianity in Africa: A Renewal of a Non-Christian Religion*. Maryknoll, NY: Orbis Books, 1995.

Bevans, Stephen B. *Models of Contextual Theology*. 2nd ed. Maryknoll, NY: Orbis Books, 2002.

Boas, Franz. *The Ethnography of Franz Boas*. Compiled and edited by Ronald P. Rohner. Chicago: University of Chicago Press, 1969.

Bockmuehl, Marcus. *Jewish Law in Gentile Churches*. Edinburgh: T&T Clark, 2000.

Bonhoeffer, Dietrich. *Ethics*. Edited by Eberhard Bethge. Translated by N. H. Smith. New York: Macmillan, 1955.

Boon-Itt, Bantoon, and Mai Boon-Itt, "Bridging Buddhist Christian Worldview: Communicating in Context for Theravada Buddhist Breakthrough." *Mission Frontiers* 36, no. 6 (2014): 15-19.

Bosch, David. *Transforming Mission: Paradigm Shifts in Mission Theology*. Maryknoll, NY: Orbis Books, 1991.

Boulton, Matthew Myer. *God Against Religion: Rethinking Christian Theology Through Worship*. Grand Rapids: Eerdmans, 2008.

Boyarin, Daniel. *The Jewish Gospels: The Story of the Jewish Christ*. New York: New Press, 2012.

———. *Dying for God: Martyrdom and the Making of Christianity and Judaism*. Stanford, CA: Stanford University Press, 1999.

Calvin, John. *Institutes of the Christian Religion*. Edited by John McNeill. Translated by Ford Lewis Battles. Philadelphia: Westminster, 1960.

Caputo, John. *The Weakness of God: A Theology of the Event*. Bloomington, IN: Indiana University Press, 2006.

Chaves, Mark. *Congregations in America*. Cambridge, MA: Harvard University Press, 2004.

Clooney, Francis X. *Comparative Theology: Deep Learning Across Religious Borders*. Malden, MA: Wiley-Blackwell, 2010.

———. "Comparative Theology." In *The Oxford Handbook of Systematic Theology*, edited by John Webster, Kathryn Tanner, and Ian Torrance, 653-69. Oxford: Oxford University Press, 2007.

Congdon, David W. *The Mission of Demythologizing: Rudolf Bultmann's Dialectic Theology*. Minneapolis: Fortress, 2015.

Davis, Ellen F. *Scripture, Culture and Agriculture: An Agrarian Reading of the Bible*. Cambridge: Cambridge University Press, 2009.

DeNeui, "A Typology of Approaches to Folk Buddhists." In *Appropriate Christianity*, edited by Charles H. Kraft, 415-36. Pasadena, CA: William Carey Library, 2005.

Duerksen, Darrin Todd. *Ecclesial Identities in a Multi-Faith Context: Jesus Truth-Gatherings (Yeshu Satsangs) Among Hindus and Sikhs in Northwest India*. Eugene, OR: Pickwick, 2015.

Flemming, Dean. *Contextualization in the New Testament: Patterns for Theology and Mission*. Downers Grove, IL: InterVarsity Press, 2005.

Dyrness, William A. *How Does America Hear the Gospel?* Grand Rapids: Eerdmans, 1989.

———."Environmental Ethics and the Covenant of Hosea 2." In *Studies in Old Testament Theology*, edited by Robert L. Hubbard, Robert K. Johnston, and Robert P. Meye, 263-78. Waco, TX: Word, 1992.

———. *Learning About Theology from the Third World*. Grand Rapids: Zondervan, 1990.

———. *The Earth Is God's: A Theology of American Culture*. Maryknoll, NY: Orbis Books, 1997.

———. *Reformed Theology and Visual Culture: The Protestant Imagination from Calvin to Edwards*. Cambridge: Cambridge University Press, 2004.

———. *Senses of the Soul: Art and Visual in Christian Worship*. Eugene, OR: Cascade, 2009.

———. *Poetic Theology: God and the Poetics of Everyday Life*. Grand Rapids: Eerdmans, 2010.

———. *Senses of Devotion: Interfaith Aesthetics in Buddhist and Muslim Communities*. Eugene, OR: Cascade, 2013.

———, and Oscar García-Johnson, *Theology Without Borders: An Introduction to Global Conversations*. Grand Rapids: Baker Academic, 2015.

Gadamer, Hans-Georg. *Truth and Method*. New York: Seabury, 1975.

Geertz, Clifford. *The Interpretation of Cultures: Selected Essays*. New York: Basic Books, 1973.

Gibbs, Eddie, and Ryan K. Bolger. *Emerging Churches: Creating Christian Community in Postmodern Cultures*. Grand Rapids: Baker Academic, 2005.

Githieya, Francis Kimani. *The Freedom of the Spirit: African Indigenous Churches in Kenya*. Atlanta: Scholars Press, 1997.

Gregory, Brad S. *The Unintended Reformation: How a Religious Revolution Secularized Society*. Cambridge, MA: Harvard University Press, 2012.

Goldingay, John. "How Does the First Testament Look at Other Religions?" In *Key Questions About Christian Faith: Old Testament Answers*, 186-99. Grand Rapids: Baker Books, 2010.

Green, Joel B., and Mark D. Baker, *Recovering the Scandal of the Cross: The Atonement in New Testament and Contemporary Contexts*. 2nd ed. Downers Grove, IL: InterVarsity Press, 2011.

———. *Practicing Theological Interpretation*. Grand Rapids: Baker Academic, 2011.

Gunton, Colin. *Act and Being: Towards a Theology of the Divine Attributes*. Grand Rapids: Eerdmans, 2002.

Halík, Tomáš. *Patience with God: The Story of Zacchaeus Continuing in Us.* Translated by Gerald Turner. New York: Doubleday, 2009.

Hanciles, Jehu. *Beyond Christendom: Globalization, African Migration and the Transformation of the West.* Maryknoll, NY: Orbis Books, 2008.

Hesselgrave, David, and Edward Rommen. *Contextualization: Meanings, Methods and Models.* Grand Rapids: Baker Books, 1989.

Hiebert, Paul G. "Critical Contextualization." *International Bulletin of Missionary Research* 11, no. 3 (1987): 104-111.

——. "The Category of Christian in the Mission Task." In *Anthropological Reflections on Missiological Issues,* 107-36. Grand Rapids: Baker Academic, 1994.

——. "Metatheology: The Step Beyond Contextualization." In *Anthropological Reflections on Missiological Issues,* 93-103. Grand Rapids: Baker Books, 1994.

——, R. Daniel Shaw, and Tite Tiénou. *Understanding Folk Religion: A Christian Response to Popular Beliefs and Practices.* Grand Rapids: Baker Academic, 1999.

Hock, Klaus. "Beyond the Multireligious—Transculturation and Religion Differentiation: In Search of a New Paradigm in the Academic Study of Religion, Church and Interreligious Encounter." In *Theology and the Religions: A Dialogue,* edited by Viggo Mortensen, 52-62. Grand Rapids: Eerdmans, 2003.

Hoefer, Herbet E. *Churchless Christianity.* Pasadena, CA: William Carey Library, 2001.

Jenkins, Philip. *The Next Christendom: The Coming of Global Christianity.* 3rd ed. New York: Oxford University Press, 2011.

Jennings, Willie James. *The Christian Imagination: Theology and the Origins of Race.* New Haven, CT: Yale University Press, 2010.

Juergensmeyer, Mark. "Introduction." In *The Oxford Handbook of Global Religion.* Edited by Mark Juergensmeyer. New York: Oxford University Press, 2006.

Kenyatta, Jomo. *Facing Mount Kenya.* 1938. Reprint, Nairobi: Heinemann Kenya, 1978.

Kirk, J. Andrew. *The Mission of Theology and Theology as Mission.* Valley Forge, PA: Trinity Press International, 1997.

Kline, Meredith. *Images of the Spirit.* Grand Rapids: Baker Books, 198.

Kraft, Charles. *Christianity in Culture: A Study of Dynamic Biblical Theologizing in Cross-Cultural Perspective.* Maryknoll, NY: Orbis Books, 1979.

——, ed., *Appropriate Christianity.* Pasadena, CA: William Carey Library, 2005.

Ladd, George Eldon. *Jesus and the Kingdom: The Eschatology of Biblical Realism.* New York: Harper & Row, 1964.

Laubach, Frank C. *The People of the Philippines: Their Religious Progress and Preparation for Spiritual Leadership in the Far East.* New York: George Doran, 1925.

Luhrmann, Tanya. *When God Talks Back: Understanding the American Evangelical Relationship with God.* New York: Knopf, 2012.

Maggay, Melba, ed. *The Gospel in Culture: Contextualization Issues Through Asian Eyes.* Manila: OMF Literature/ISACC, 2013.

Mahmood, Saba. *Politics of Piety: The Islamic Revival and the Feminist Subject.* Princeton, NJ: Princeton University Press, 2005.

Menocal, Maria Rosa. *The Ornament of the World: How Muslims, Jews, and Christians Created a Culture of Tolerance in Medieval Spain.* Boston: Little, Brown, 2002.

Miller, Patrick D. *Israelite Religion and Biblical Theology.* Sheffield: Sheffield Academic Press, 2000.

Moffett, Samuel H. *A History of Christianity in Asia.* Vol. 1. San Francisco: Harper, 1992.

Moreau, A. Scott. *Contextualization in World Missions: Mapping and Assessing Evangelical Models.* Grand Rapids: Kregel, 2012.

Muck, Terry C., and Frances S. Adeney, *Christianity Encountering World Religions: The Practice of Mission in the Twenty-First Century.* Grand Rapids: Baker Academic, 2009.

Muir, Edward. *Ritual in Early Modern Europe.* Cambridge: Cambridge University Press, 1997.

Ortner, Sherry B. "Theory in Anthropology Since the Sixties." *Comparative Studies in Society and History* 26 (January 1984): 126-66.

Nazir-Ali, Michael. "Longing for Community: Church, Ummah, or Somewhere Between? A Review Essay." *International Bulletin of Missionary Research* 39, no. 1 (2015).

Nicholls, Bruce J. *Contextualization: A Theology of Gospel and Culture.* Downers Grove, IL: InterVarsity Press, 1979.

Oden, Patrick. *The Transformative Church: New Ecclesial Models and the Theology of Jürgen Moltmann.* Minneapolis: Fortress, 2015.

Peace, Richard V. *Conversion in the New Testament: Paul and the Twelve.* Grand Rapids: Eerdmans, 1999.

Ray, J. D. "Egyptian Wisdom Literature." In *Wisdom in Ancient Israel: Essays in Honor of J. A. Emerton,* edited by John Day, Robert P. Gordon, and H. G. M. Williamson, 17-29. Cambridge: Cambridge University Press, 1995.

Redford, Shawn B. "Appropriate Hermeneutics." In *Appropriate Christianity,* edited by Charles H. Kraft, 227-29. Pasadena, CA: William Carey Library, 2005.

Richards, H. L. "Religious Syncretism as a Syncretistic Concept: The Inadequacy of the 'World Religions' Paradigm in Cross-Cultural Encounter." In *Understanding Insider Movements,* edited by Harley Talman and John Jay Travis, 163-74. Pasadena, CA: William Carey Library, 2015.

Richardson, Don. *Peace Child.* 4th ed. Ventura, CA: Regal Books, 2005.

Ringgren, Helmer. *Israelite Religion.* Translated by David E. Green. Philadelphia: Fortress, 1966.

Roberts, Michelle Voss. *Tastes of the Divine: Hindu and Christian Theologies of Emotion.* New York: Fordham University Press, 2014.

Romaine, James. *Objects of Grace: Conversations on Creativity & Faith.* Baltimore: Square Halo Books, 2002.

Schreiter, Robert. *Constructing Local Theologies.* Maryknoll, NY: Orbis Books, 1985.

———. *The New Catholicity: Theology Between the Global and the Local.* Maryknoll, NY: Orbis Books, 1997.

Shaw, R. Daniel. "Beyond Contextualization: Toward a Twenty-First-Century Model for Enabling Mission," *International Bulletin of Missionary Research* 34, no. 4 (2010): 208-215.

Singh, Sadhu Sundar. *With and Without Christ.* New York: Harper, 1929.

Skarsaune, Oskar. *In the Shadow of the Temple: Jewish Influences on Early Christianity.* Downers Grove, IL: InterVarsity Press, 2002.

———, and Reidar Hvalvik, eds. *Jewish Believers in Jesus: The Early Centuries.* Peabody, MA: Hendrickson, 2007.

Smith, Christian. *To Flourish or Destruct: A Personalist Theory of Human Goods, Motivations, Failure, and Evil.* Chicago: University of Chicago Press, 2015.

Smilde, David. *Reason to Believe: Cultural Agency in Latin American Evangelicalism.* Berkeley: University of California Press, 2007.

Smith, David. *Mission After Christendom.* London: Darton, Longman & Todd, 2003.

Smith, Wilfred Cantwell. *The Meaning and End of Religion: A New Approach to the Religious Traditions of Mankind.* New York: Macmillan, 1963.

Stackhouse, Max. *Apologia: Contextualization, Globalization and Mission in Theological Education.* Grand Rapids: Eerdmans, 1988.

Stott, John R. W., and Robert T. Coote. *Down to Earth: Essays in Gospel and Culture.* Grand Rapids: Eerdmans, 1980.

Sundermeier, Theo. *Was ist Religion? Religionswissenshaft im theologischen Kontext: ein Studienbuch.* Gütersloh: Gütersloh Verlagshaus, 1999.

Sunquist, Scott W. *Understanding Christian Mission: Participation in Suffering and Glory.* Grand Rapids: Baker Academic, 2013.

Talman, Harley, and John Jay Travis, eds. *Understanding Insider Movements: Disciples of Jesus Within Diverse Religious Communities.* Pasadena, CA: William Carey Library, 2015.

Tamez, Elsa. "Reliving Our Histories: Racial and Cultural Revelations of God." In *New Vision for the Americas: Religious Engagement and Social Transformation,* edited by David Batstone, 33-56. Minneapolis: Augsburg Fortress, 1994.

Tan, Jonathan. *Christian Mission Among the Peoples of Asia.* Maryknoll, NY: Orbis Books, 2014.

Tan, Kang-San. "Beyond Demonising Religions: A Biblical Framework for Interfaith Relations in Asia." *Church and Society in Asia Today* 15 (2012): 185-96.

——. "An Examination of Dual Religious Belonging Theology: Contributions to Evangelical Missiology." PhD diss., University of Aberdeen, 2014.

Tanner, Kathryn. *Theories of Culture: A New Agenda for Theology*. Minneapolis: Fortress, 1997.

Taves, Ann. "'Religion' in the Humanities and the Humanities in the University." *Journal of the American Academy of Religion* 79, no. 2 (2011): 287-314.

——. *Religious Experience Reconsidered: A Building-Block Approach to the Study of Religion and Other Special Things*. Princeton, NJ: Princeton University Press, 2009.

Taylor, Charles. *Sources of the Self: The Making of the Modern Identity*. Cambridge, MA: Harvard University Press, 1989.

——. *A Secular Age*. Cambridge, MA: Harvard University Press, 2007.

Tennent, Timothy. *Theology in the Context of World Christianity: How the Global Church Is Influencing the Way We Think About and Discuss Theology*. Grand Rapids: Zondervan, 2007.

Thomas, M. M. *Salvation and Humanisation: Some Crucial Issues of the Theology of Mission in Contemporary India*. Madras: Christian Institute on the Study of Religion and Society, 1971.

Travis, Anna. "In the World but Not of It: Insider Movements and Freedom from the Demonic." In *Understanding Insider Movements*, edited by Harley Talman and John Jay Travis, 521-36. Pasadena, CA: William Carey Library, 2015.

Travis, John. "The C1 to C6 Spectrum." *Evangelical Missions Quarterly* 34, no. 4 (1998): 407-8.

Van Gelder, Craig. *The Essence of the Church: A Community Created by the Spirit*. Grand Rapids: Baker Books, 2000.

Volf, Miroslav, ed. *Do We Worship the Same God? Jews, Christians and Muslims in Dialogue*. Grand Rapids: Eerdmans, 2012.

——. *Allah: A Christian Response*. New York: HarperOne, 2011.

Walls, Andrew. "The Rise of Global Theologies." In *Global Theology in Evangelical Perspective: Exploring the Contextual Nature of Theology and Mission*, edited by Jeffrey P. Greenman and Gene L. Green. Downers Grove, IL: InterVarsity Press, 2012.

——. "The Gospel as the Prisoner and Liberator of Culture." *Missionalia* 10, no. 4 (1982): 93-105.

Wetchgama, Banpote. "The New Buddhists: How Buddhists Can Follow Christ." *Mission Frontiers* 36, no. 6 (2014): 28-31.

Wheeler, Jesse. "'Is Allah God?' Five Reasons I Am Convinced." In *Understanding*

Insider Movements, edited by Harley Talman and John Jay Travis, 517-19. Pasadena, CA: William Carey Library, 2015.

Williams, A. N. "The Theology of the Comedy." In *Cambridge Companion to Dante*, edited by Rachel Jacoff, 2nd ed., 201-17. Cambridge: Cambridge University Press, 2007.

Williams, Rowan. *On Christian Theology*. New York: Blackwell, 2000.

Wolterstorff, Nicholas. *Justice: Rights and Wrongs*. Princeton, NJ: Princeton University Press, 2008.

Woodberry, J. Dudley. "Contextualization Among Muslims: Reusing Common Pillars." In *Understanding Insider Movements*, edited by Harley Talman and John Jay Travis, 407-35. Pasadena, CA: William Carey Library, 2015.

Woodberry, Robert D. "The Missionary: Roots of Liberal Democracy." *American Political Science Review* 106 (May 2012): 244-74.

Yong, Amos. "Francis X. Clooney's Dual Religious Belonging and the Comparative Theological Enterprise: Engaging Hindu Traditions." *Dharma Deepika: A South Asian Journal of Missiological Research* 16, no. 1 (2012): 6-26.

———. *Hospitality and the Other: Pentecost, Christian Practices and the Neighbor*. Maryknoll, NY: Orbis Books, 2008.

GENERAL INDEX

SCRIPTURE INDEX

Finding the Textbook You Need

The IVP Academic Textbook Selector
is an online tool for instantly finding the IVP books
suitable for over 250 courses across 24 disciplines.

www.ivpress.com/academic/